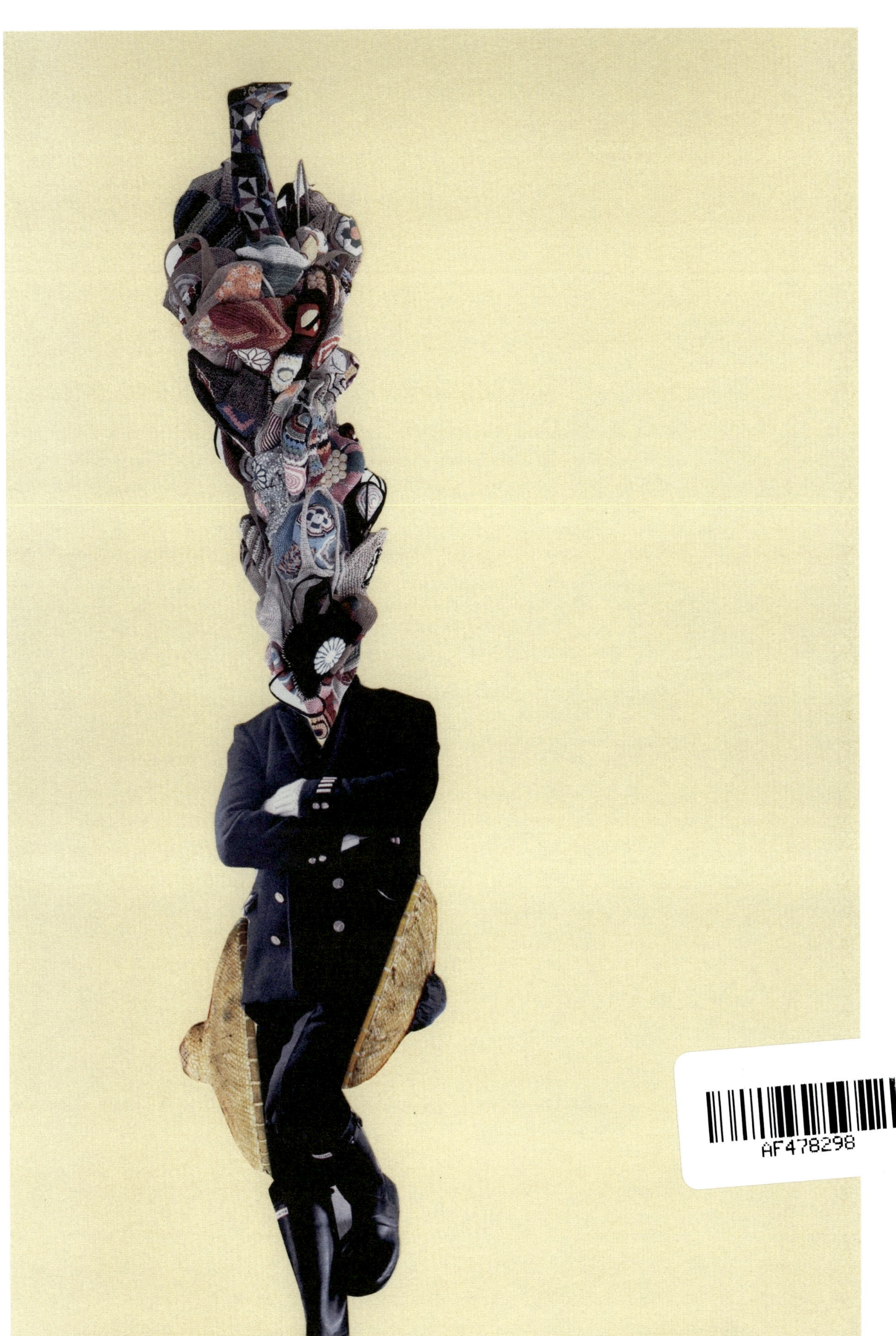

THE ICE PLANT   Los Angeles   2013

UNIFORMS

Bettina Hubby

text
by
Dave Cull

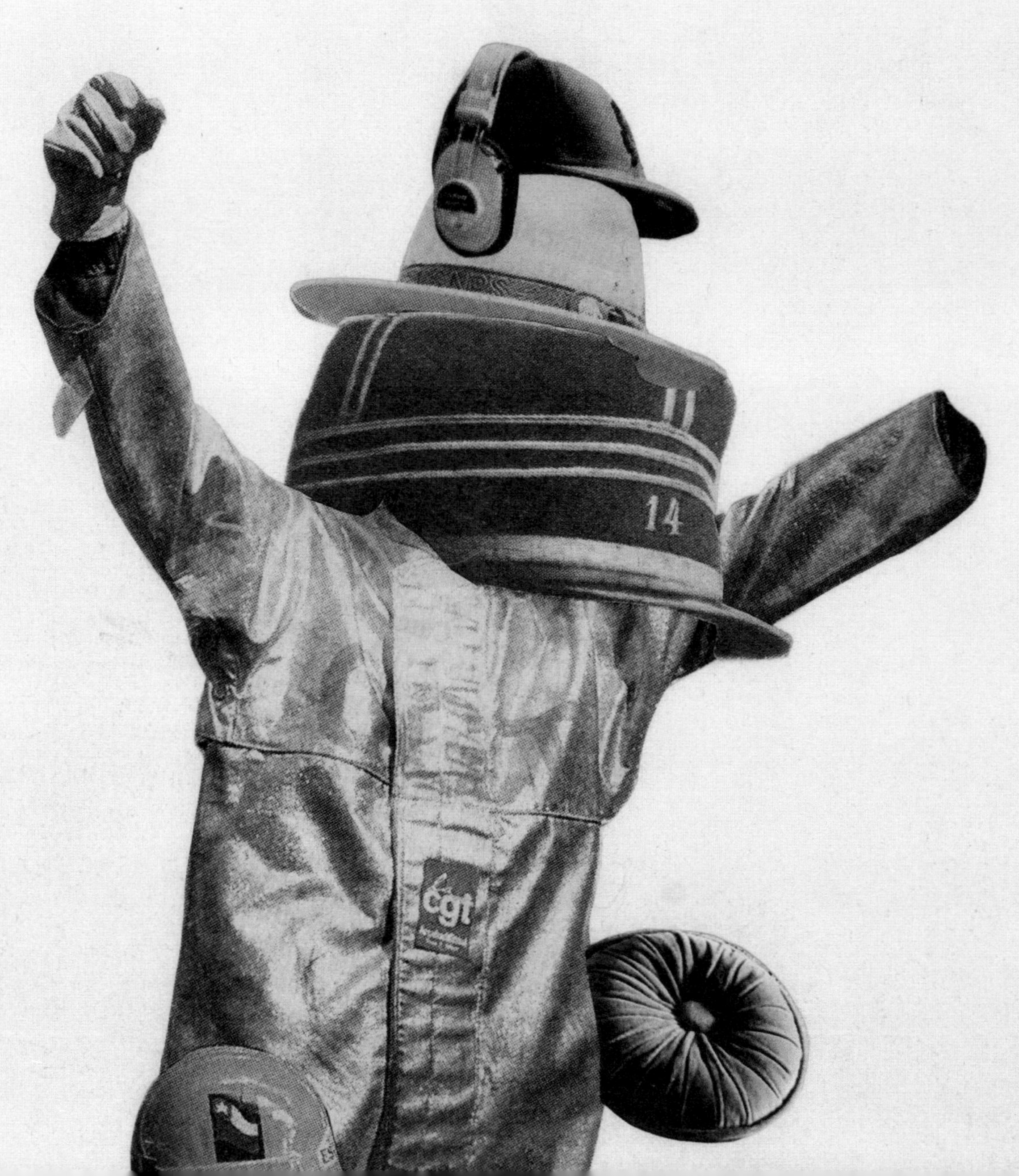

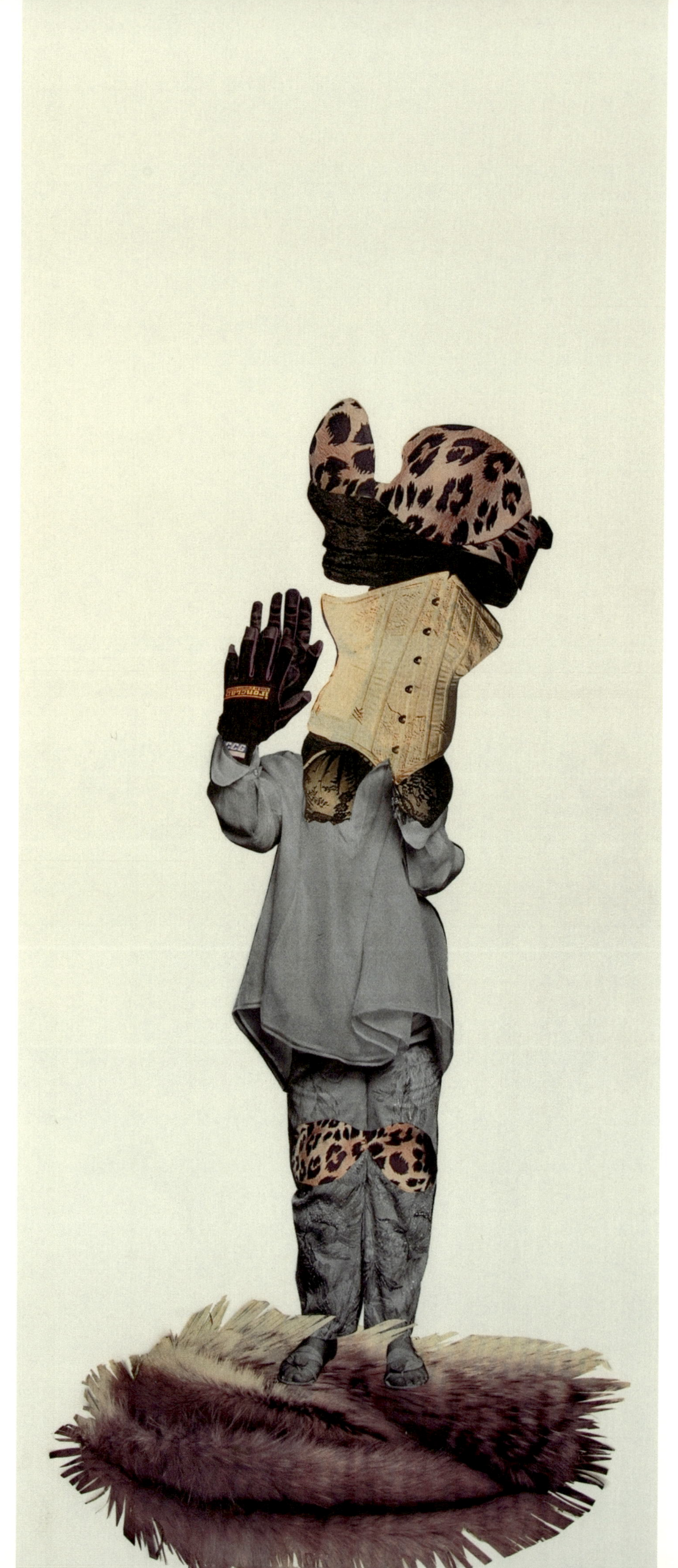

I know some people wake up immobile, entombed—their senses terribly intact. And others are aware and present for the process—the slow loss of feeling, making its way from foot to head. Either way, they sense their world, or fade to black. My experience was different.

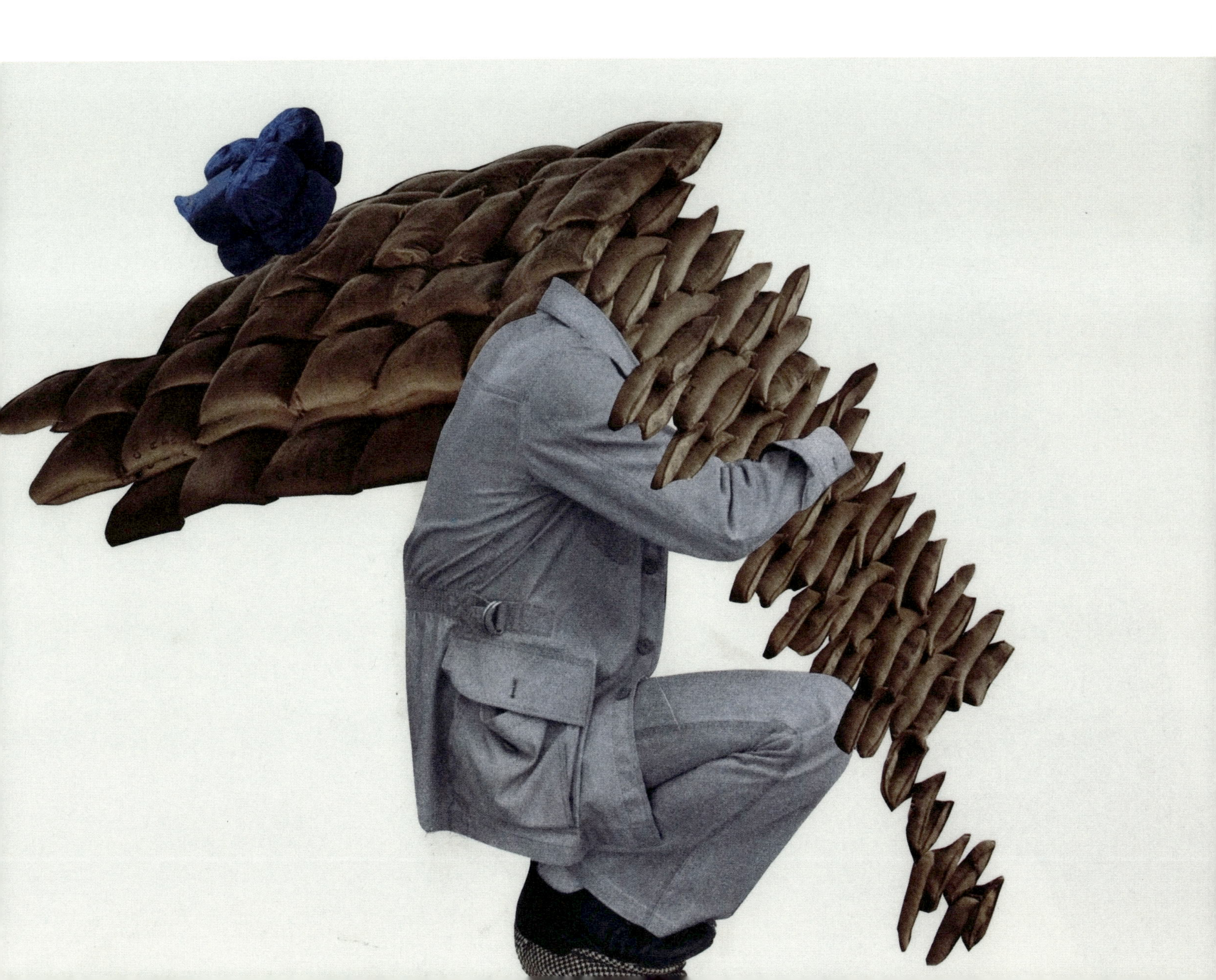

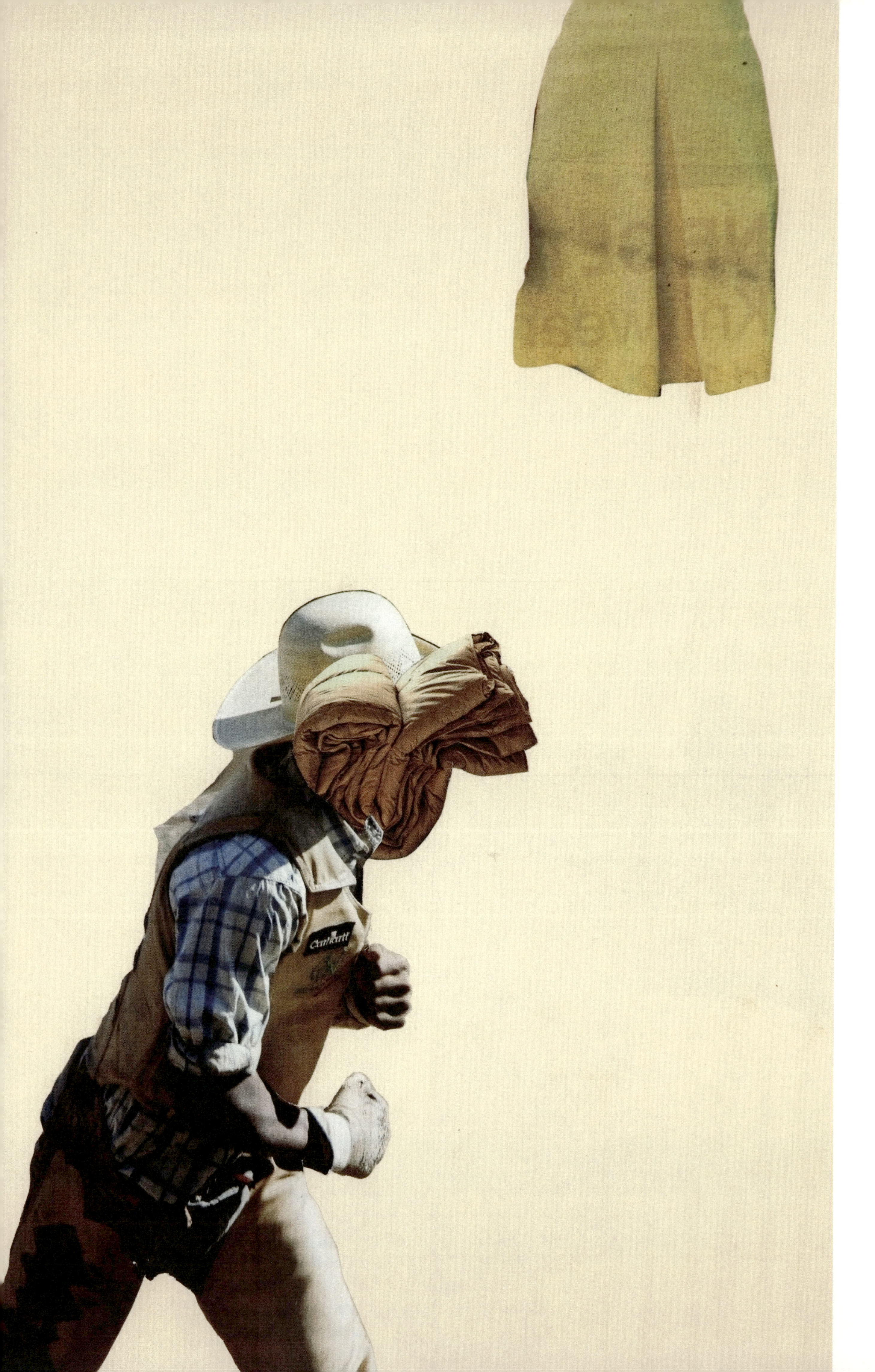

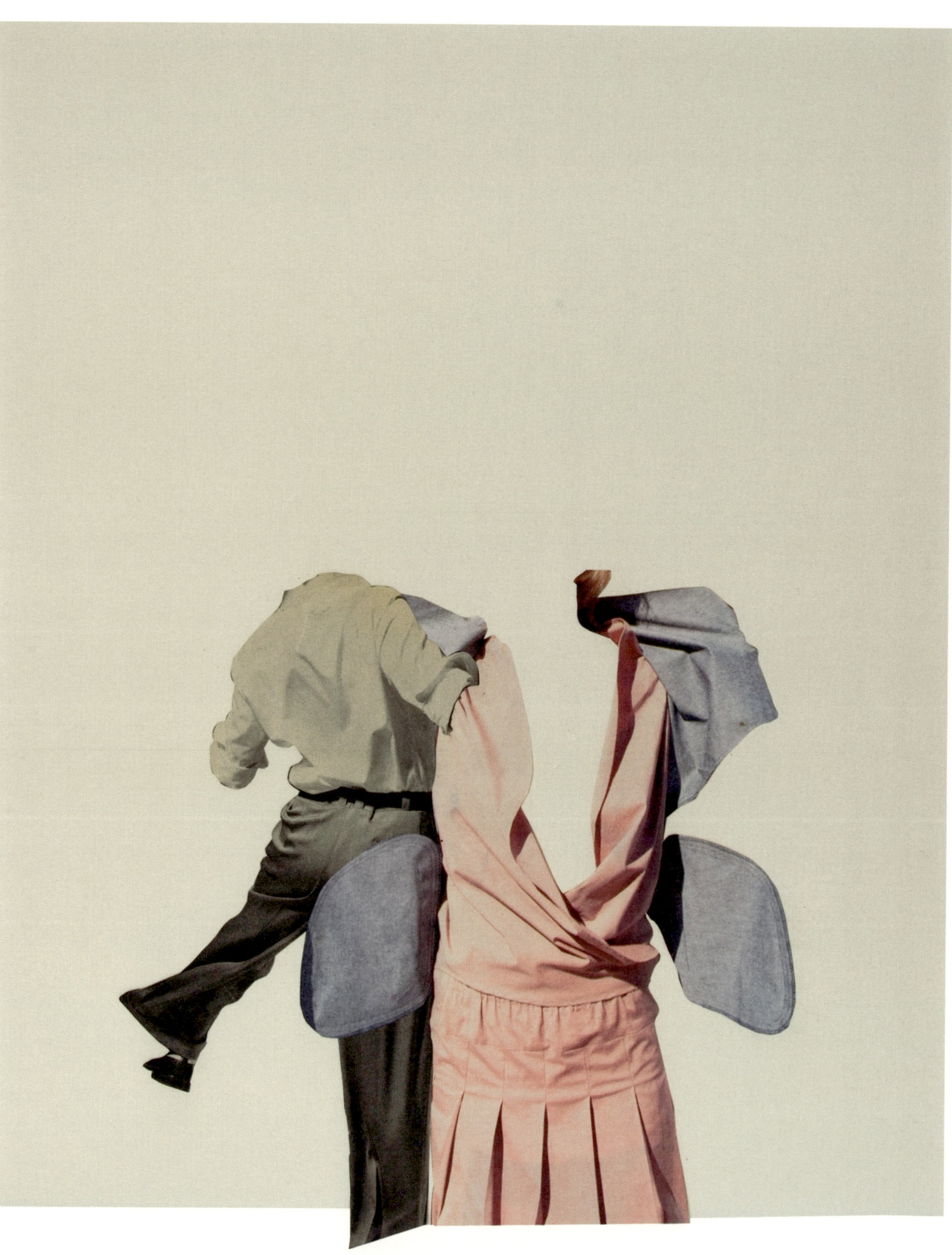

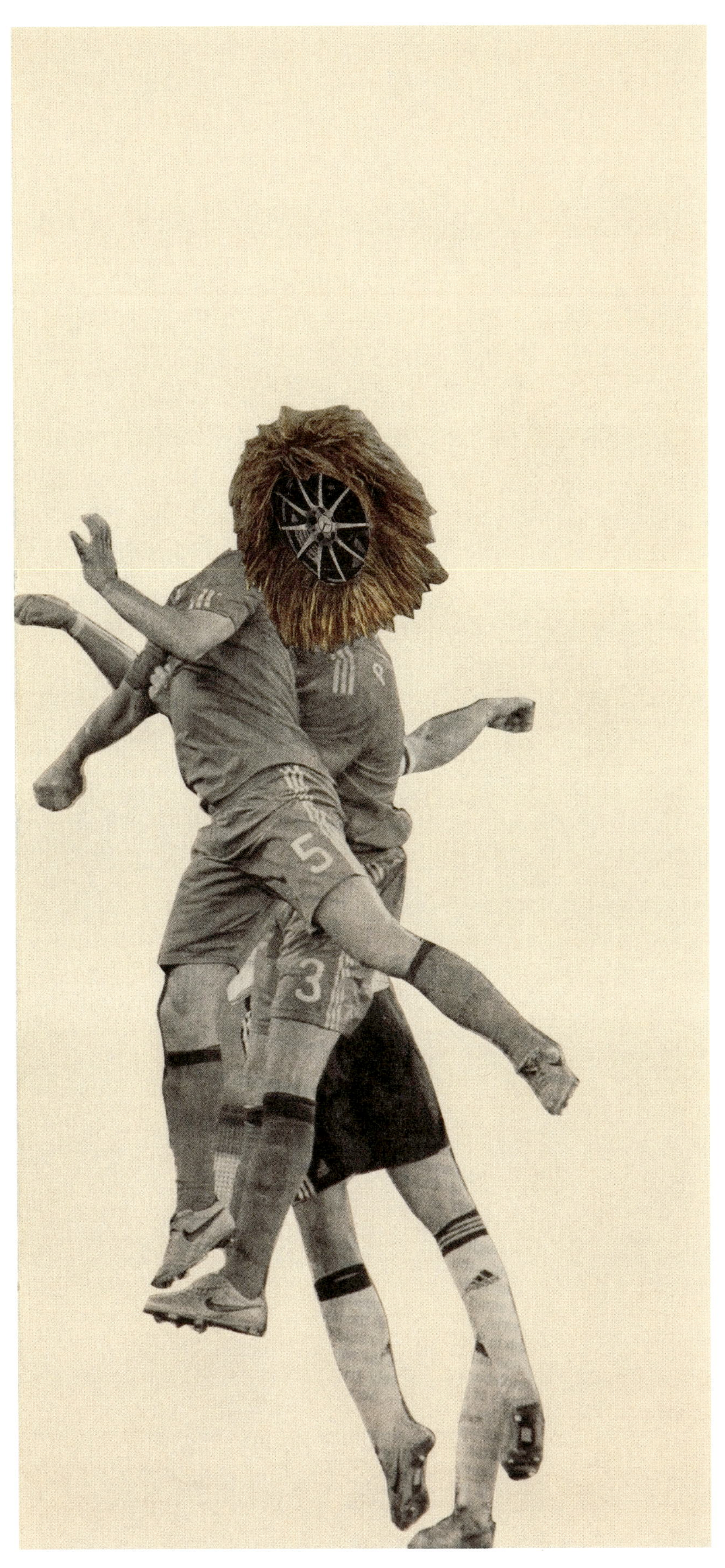

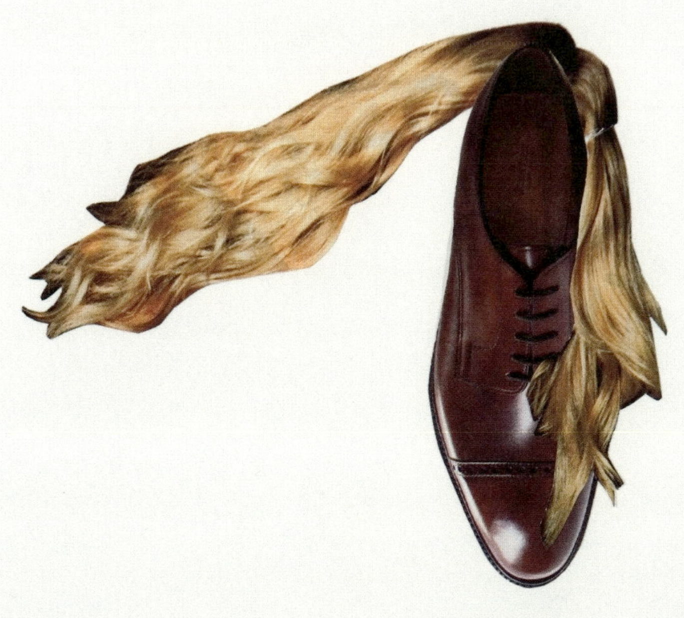

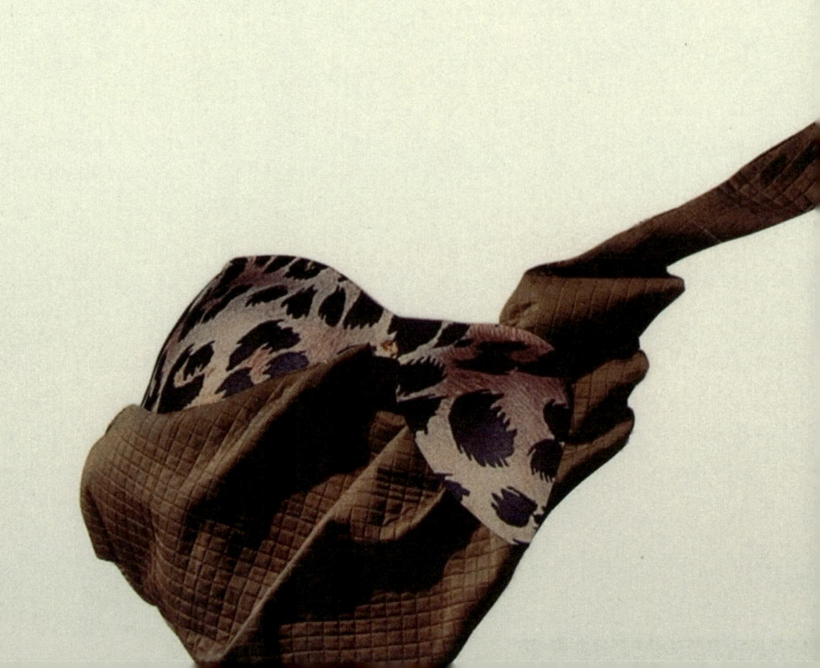

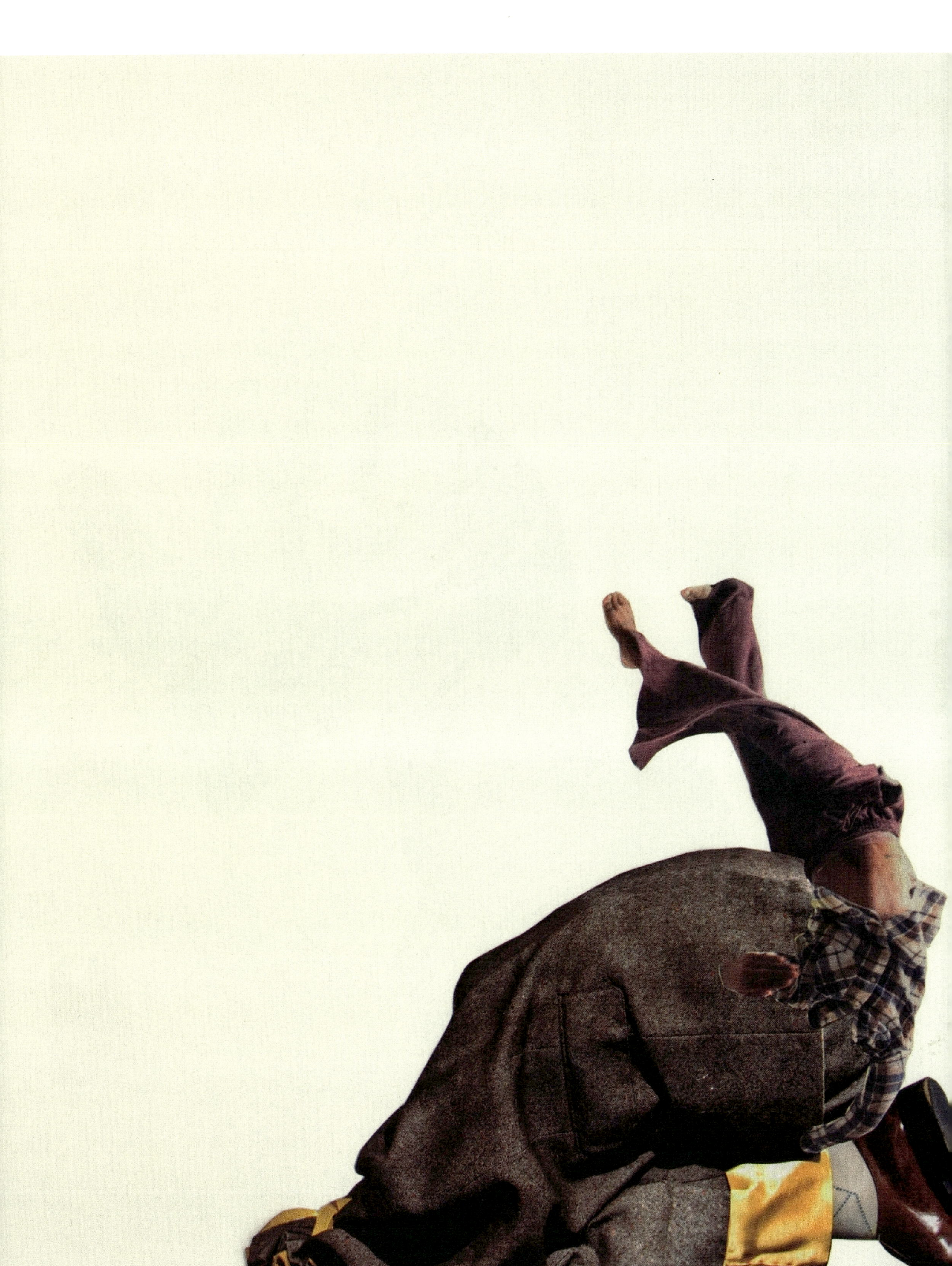

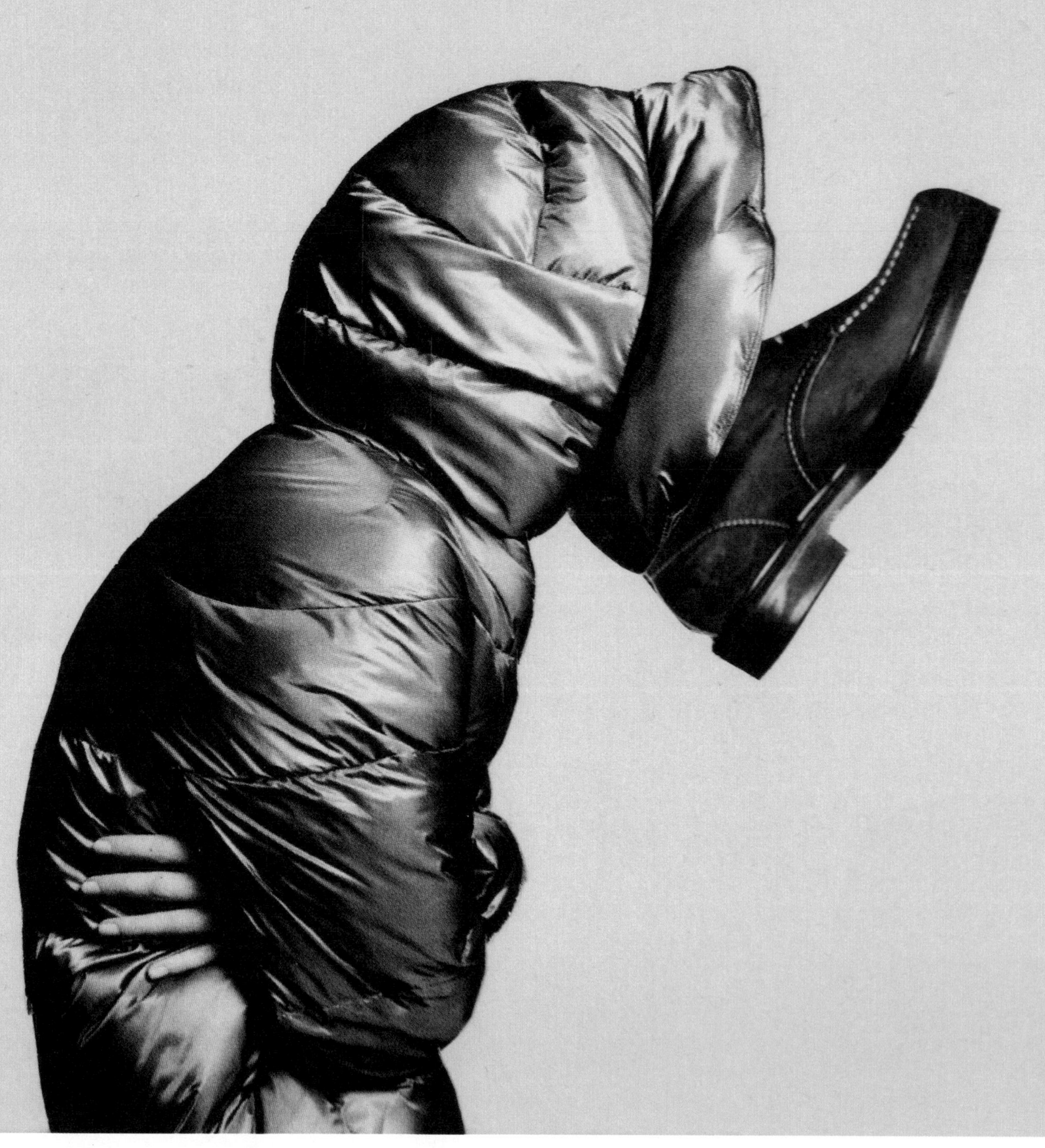

First my sight dimmed and disappeared in a matter of minutes. For a few more, I heard my voice calling out and only the mundane, disinterested sounds of daily life calling back. When taste and smell went, I wouldn't know. They were the least of my worries. I searched desperately for the phone but stumbled, instead, on a pile of laundry. I couldn't move. I expected, then, for feeling to go and death to follow. I was sure of it. I waited for it and felt that I was fading, for a moment, gone. But what happened is more improbable than death. I found myself in a new existence.

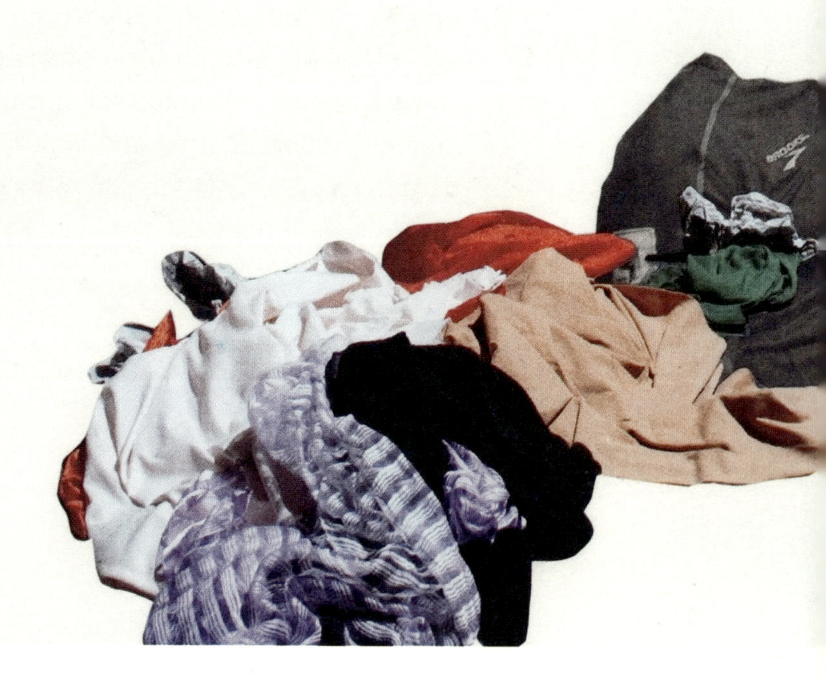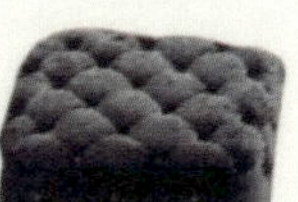

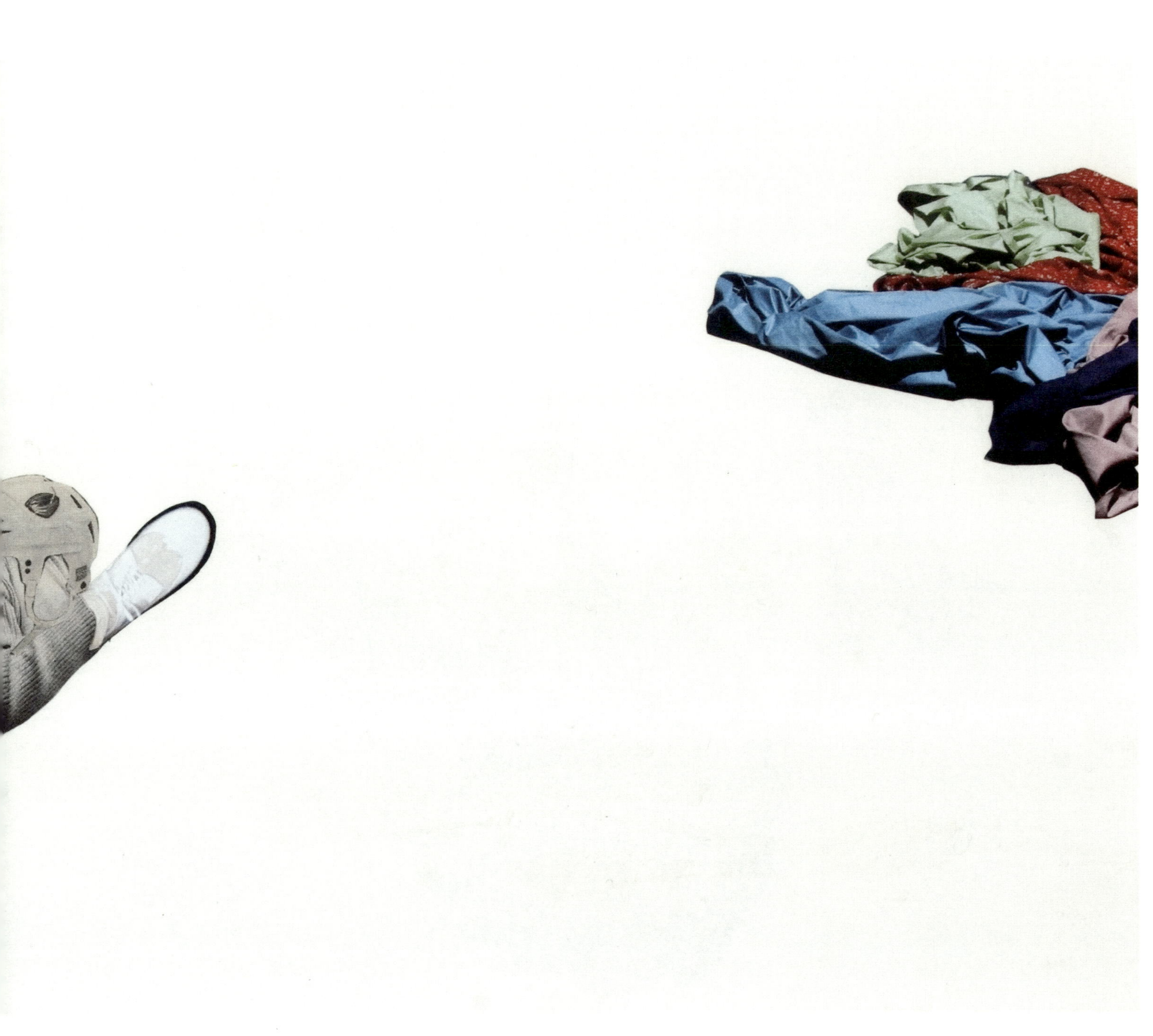

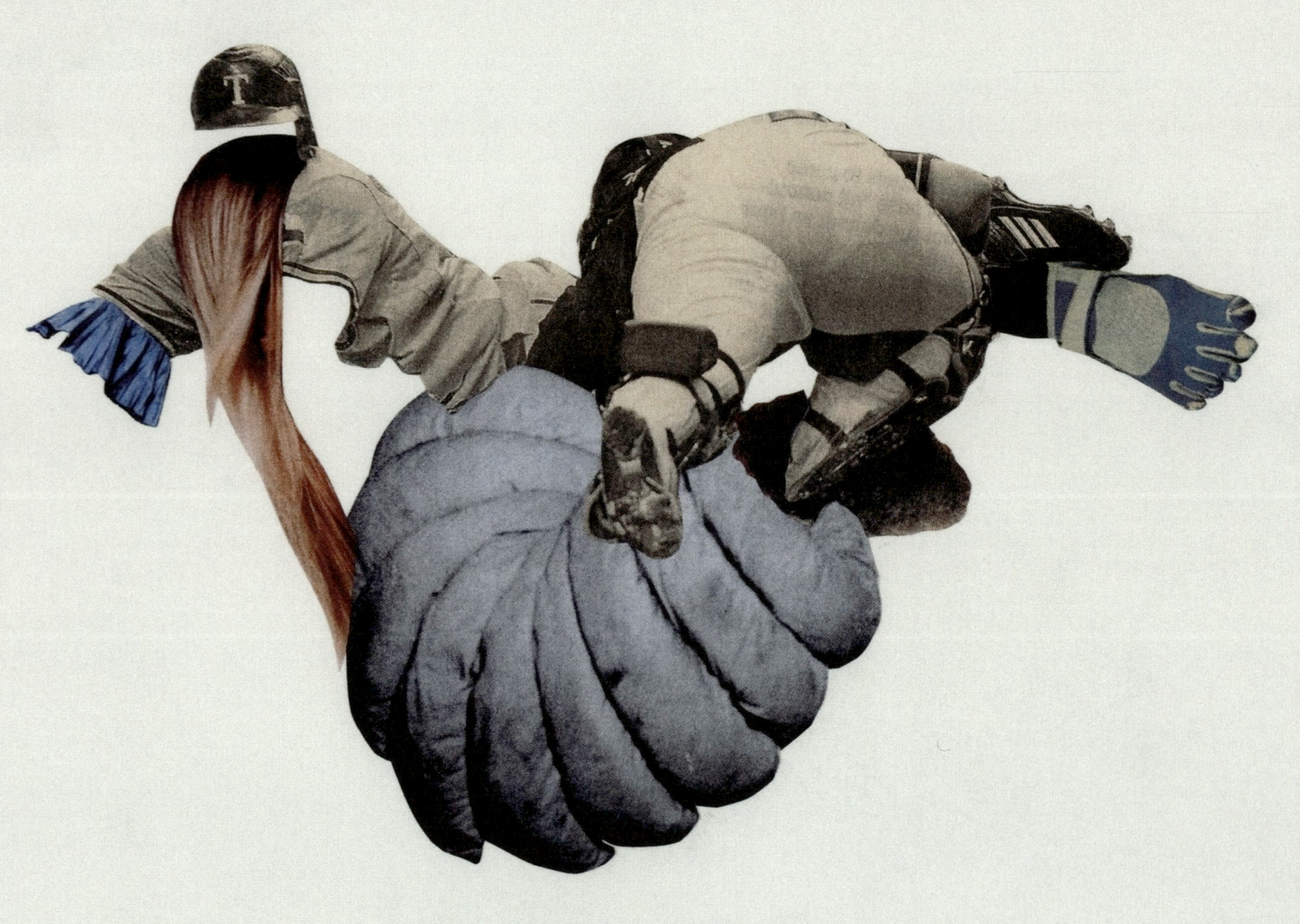

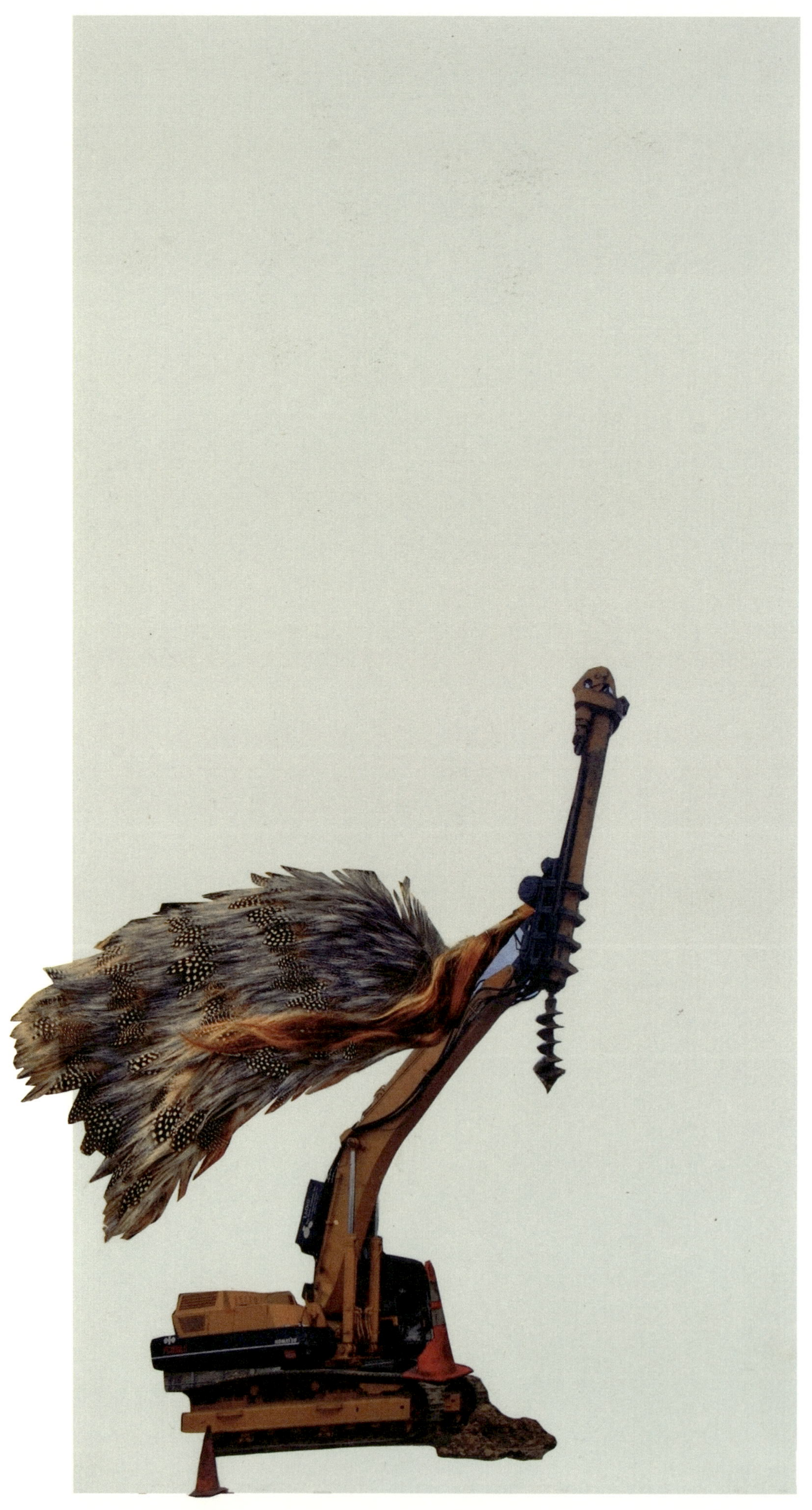

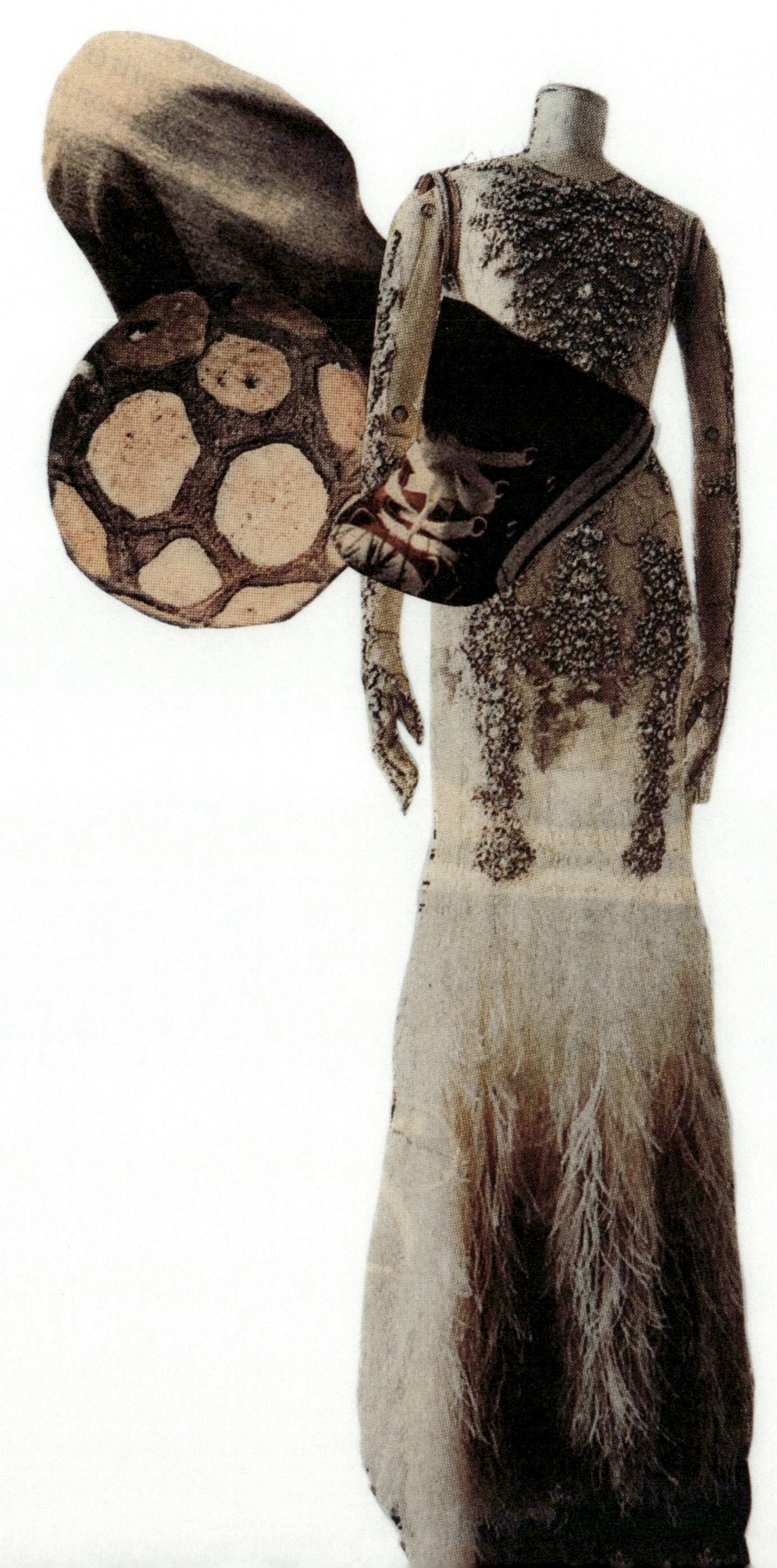

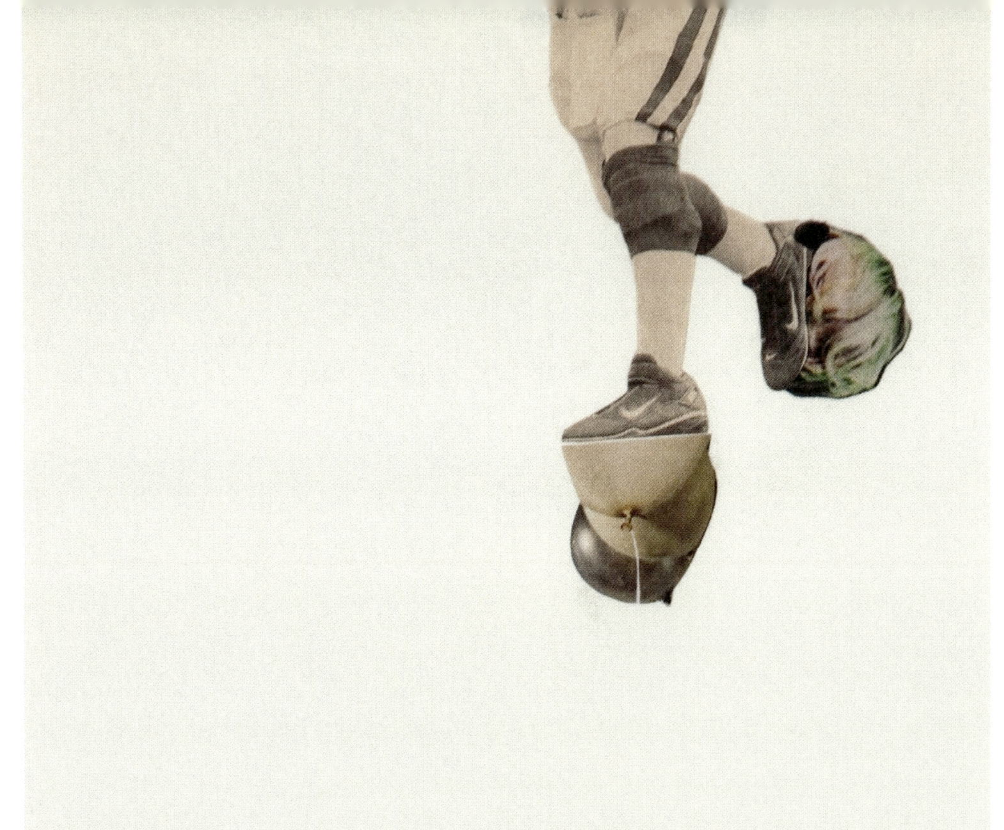

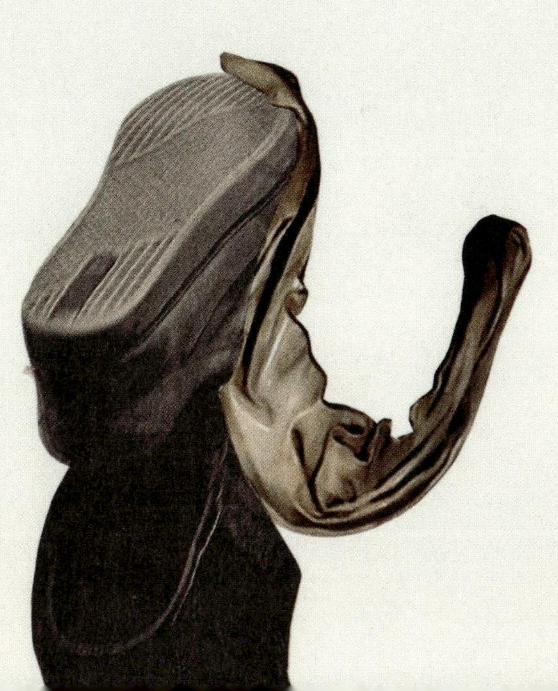

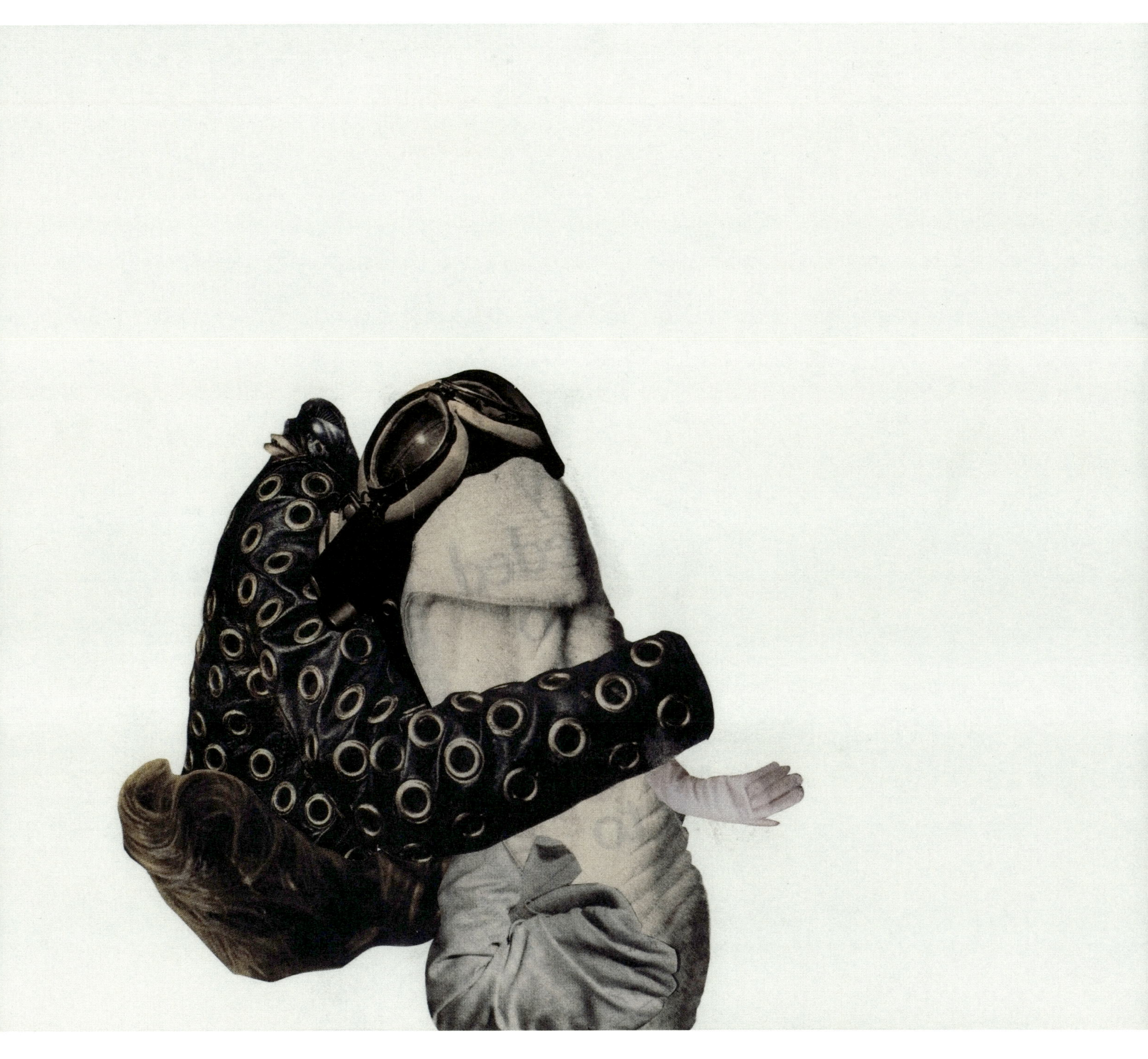

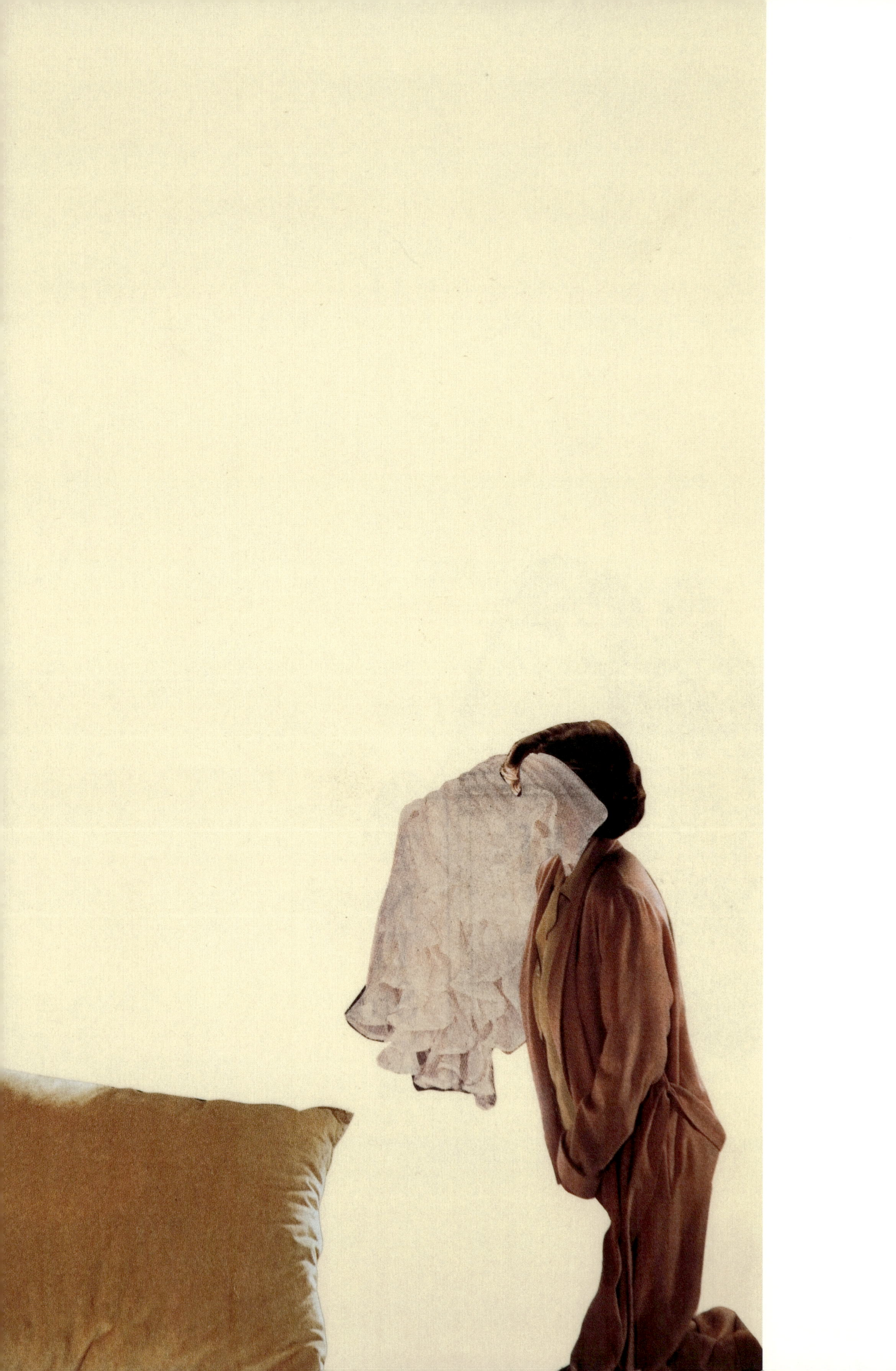

It emerged from nothing, but it emerged from me. I witnessed it, and also *was* it. I had no proprioception, per se. No volition either. I was an explosion of chaos and the rapid emergence of new qualities. A seemingly endless array came in and out of focus. Actions and interactions gave way to forms and patterns. Smaller forms—weaves and folds—led to larger ones—swaths and linings—and further on to pants, shirts, belts and shoes. Silk was an upward speed. Cotton reeled. Later, hats clung and congregated.

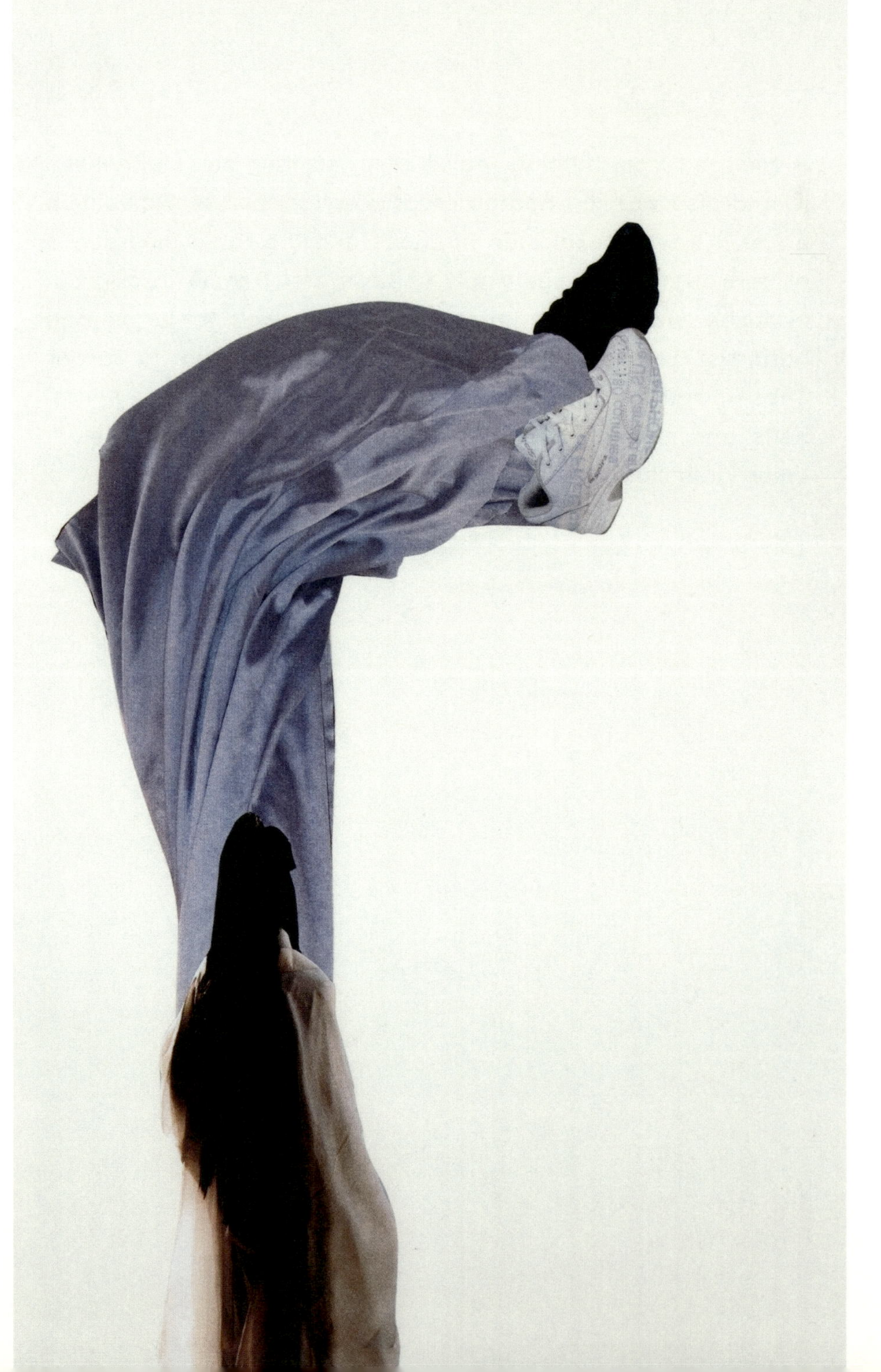

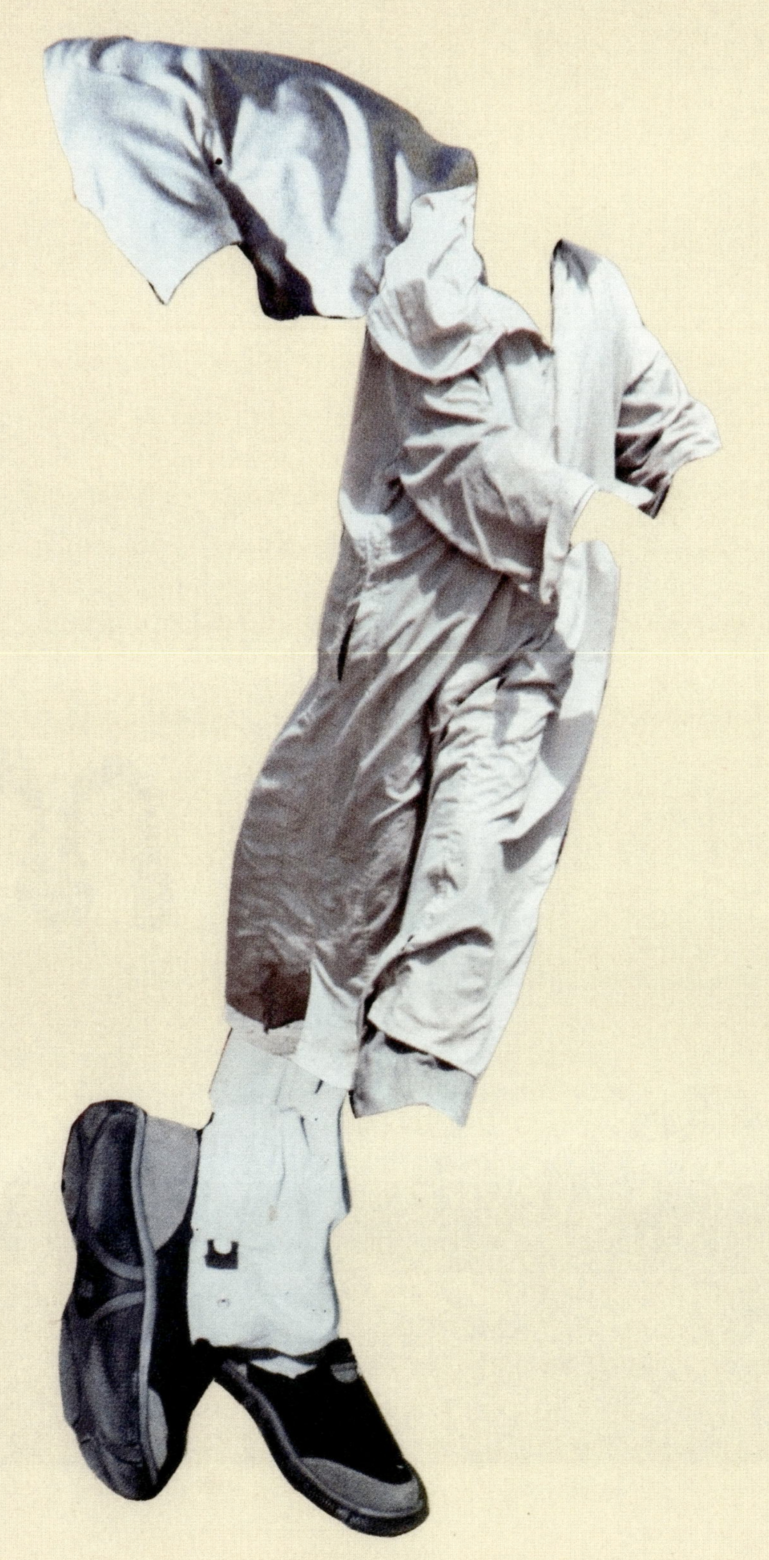

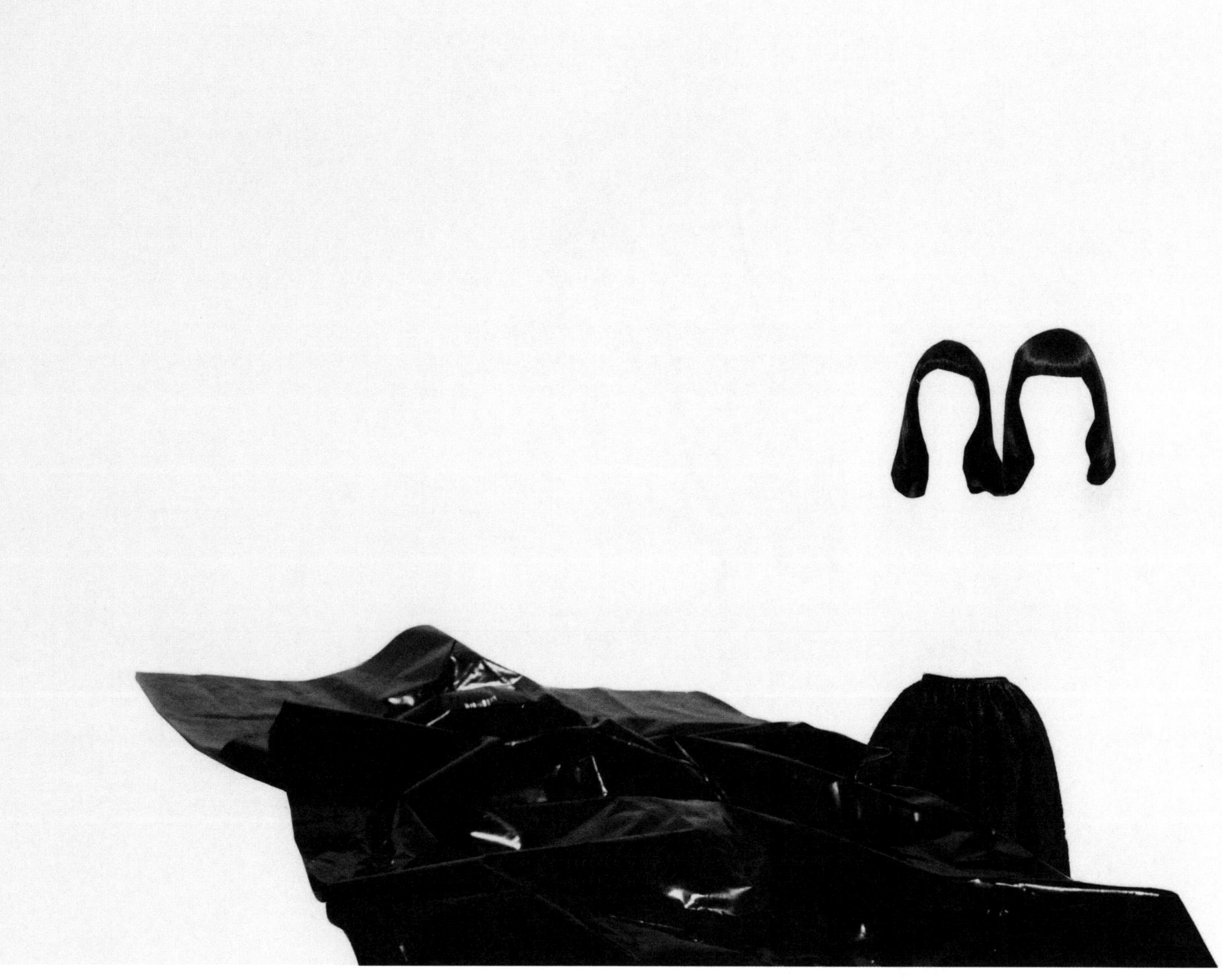

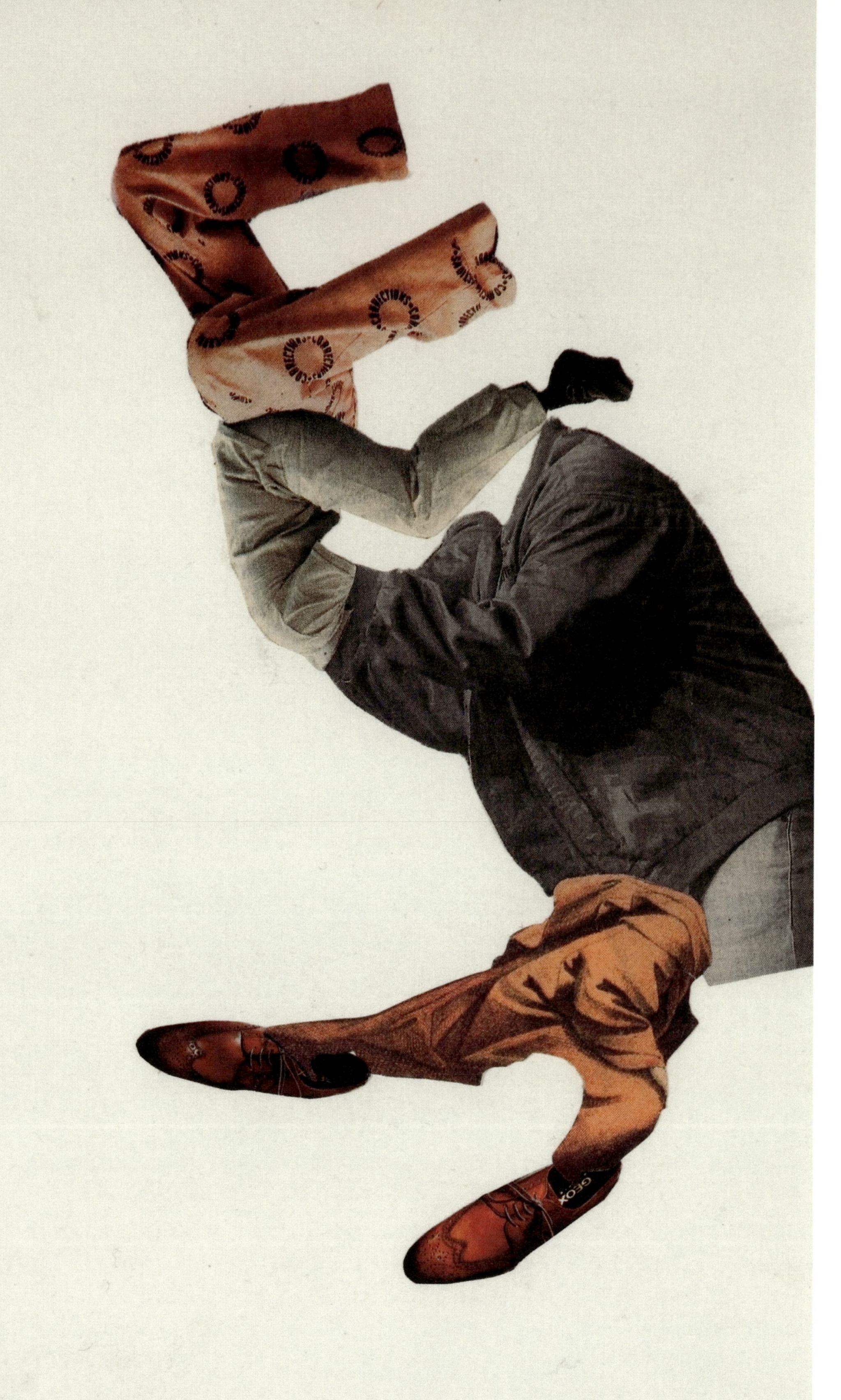

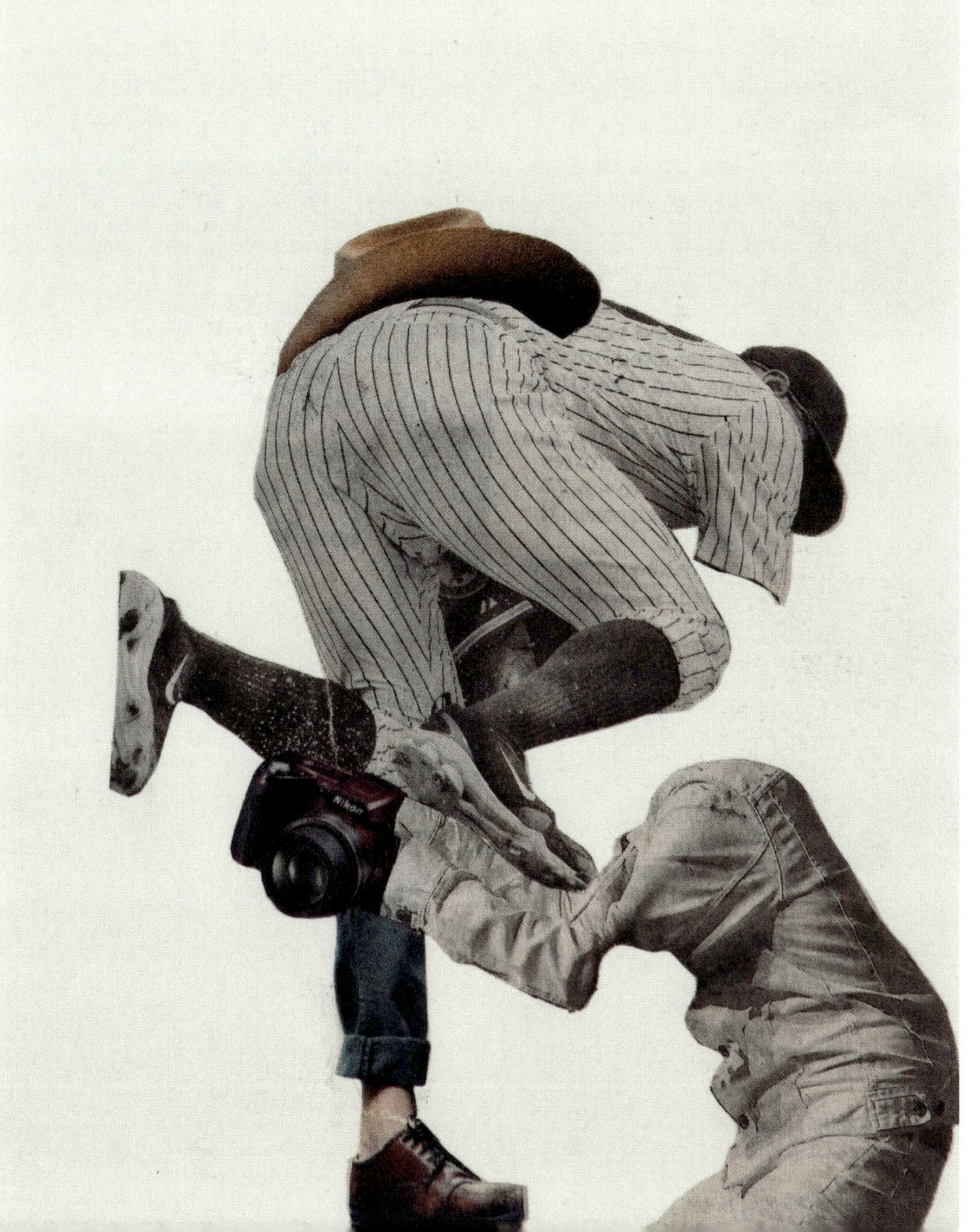

This isn't a world minus everything but clothes. This is a universe where everything is being and becoming clothes. Everything is cloth*ing*. It isn't static, orderly, or even serene. Leather likes to suffocate, gloves go after the weak, and shoes fornicate with abandon. There are dances of a kind, and battles, too. Expansions, clusters and collapses are constant. It's a kinesthetic mess.

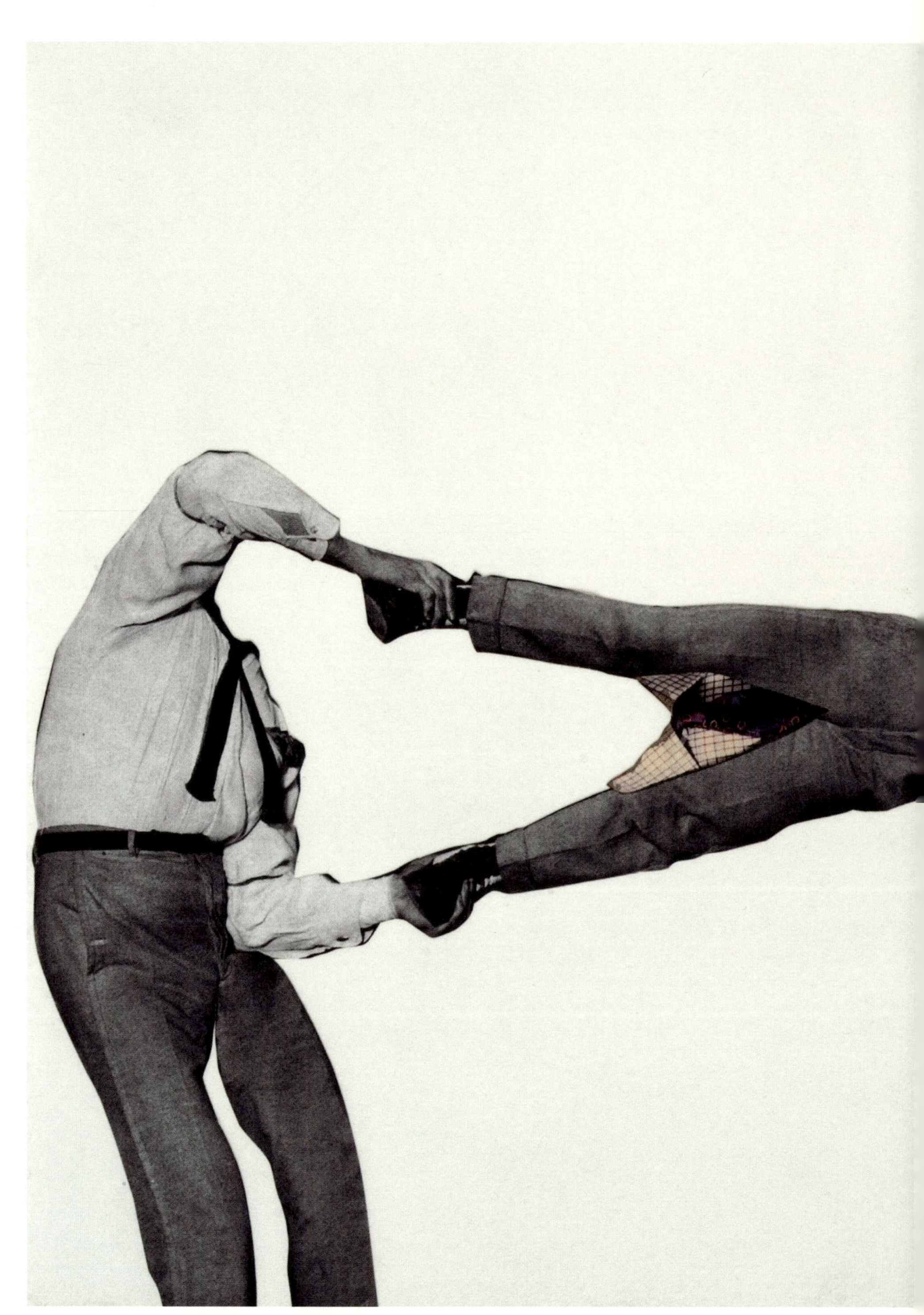

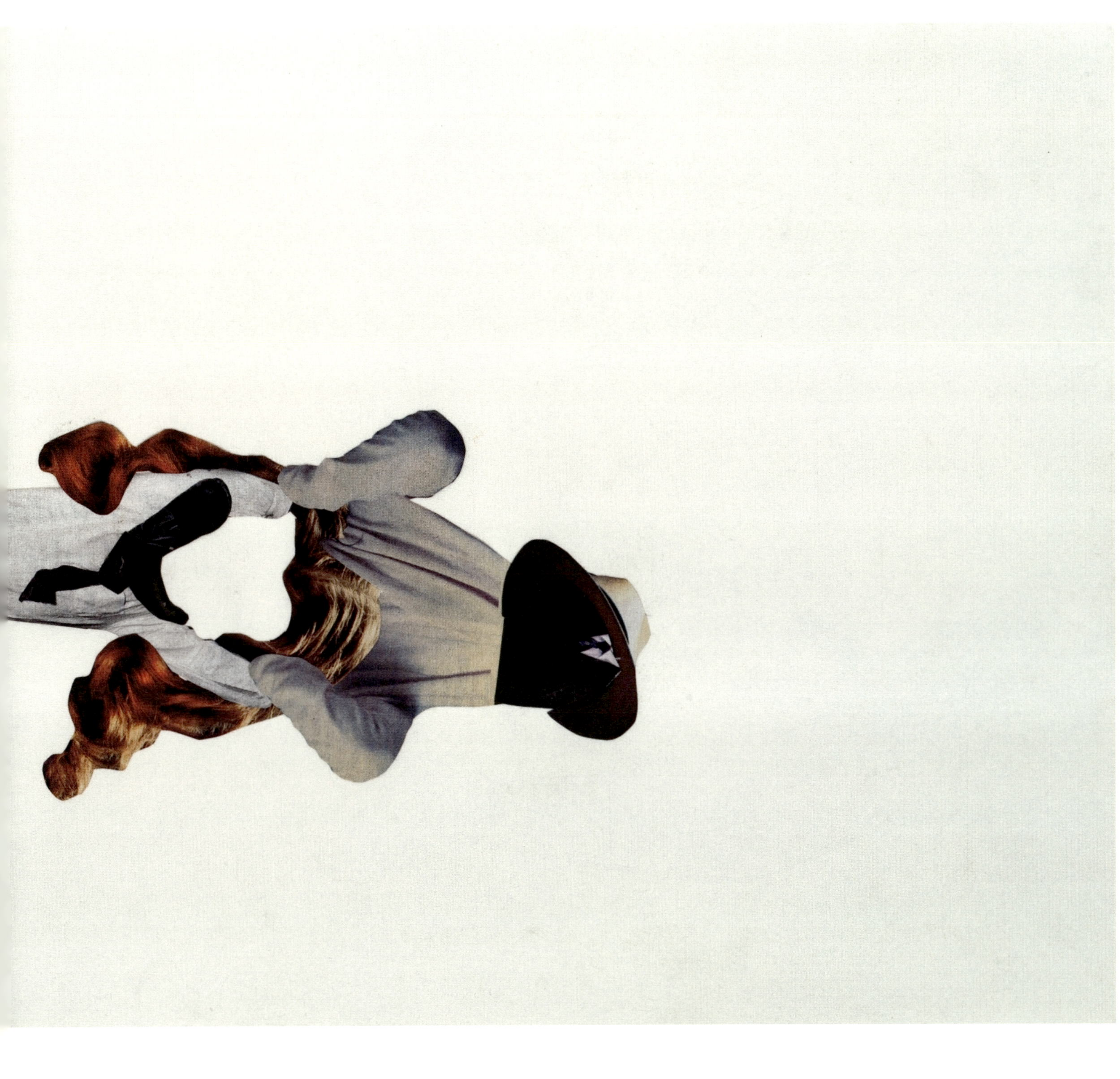

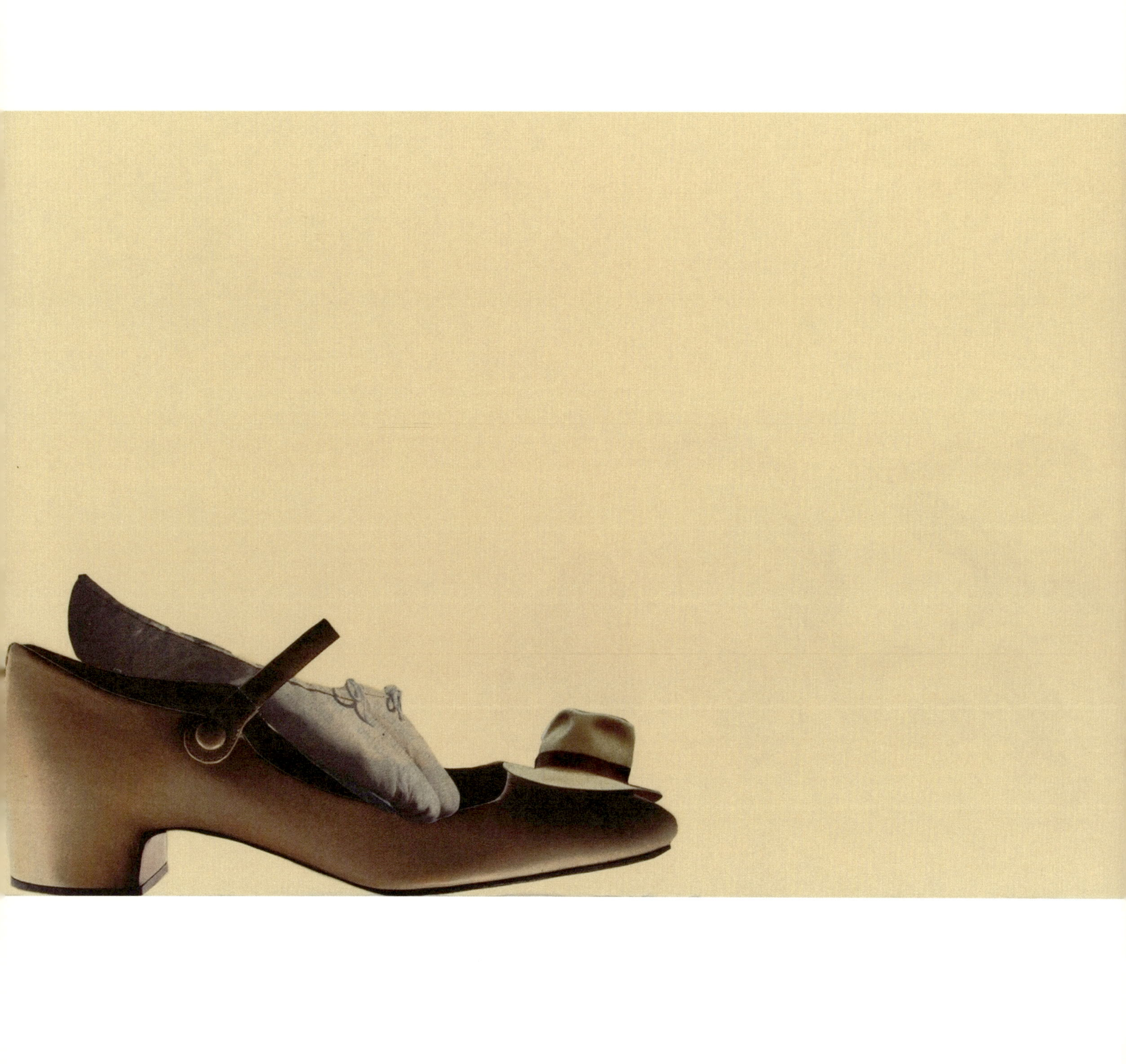

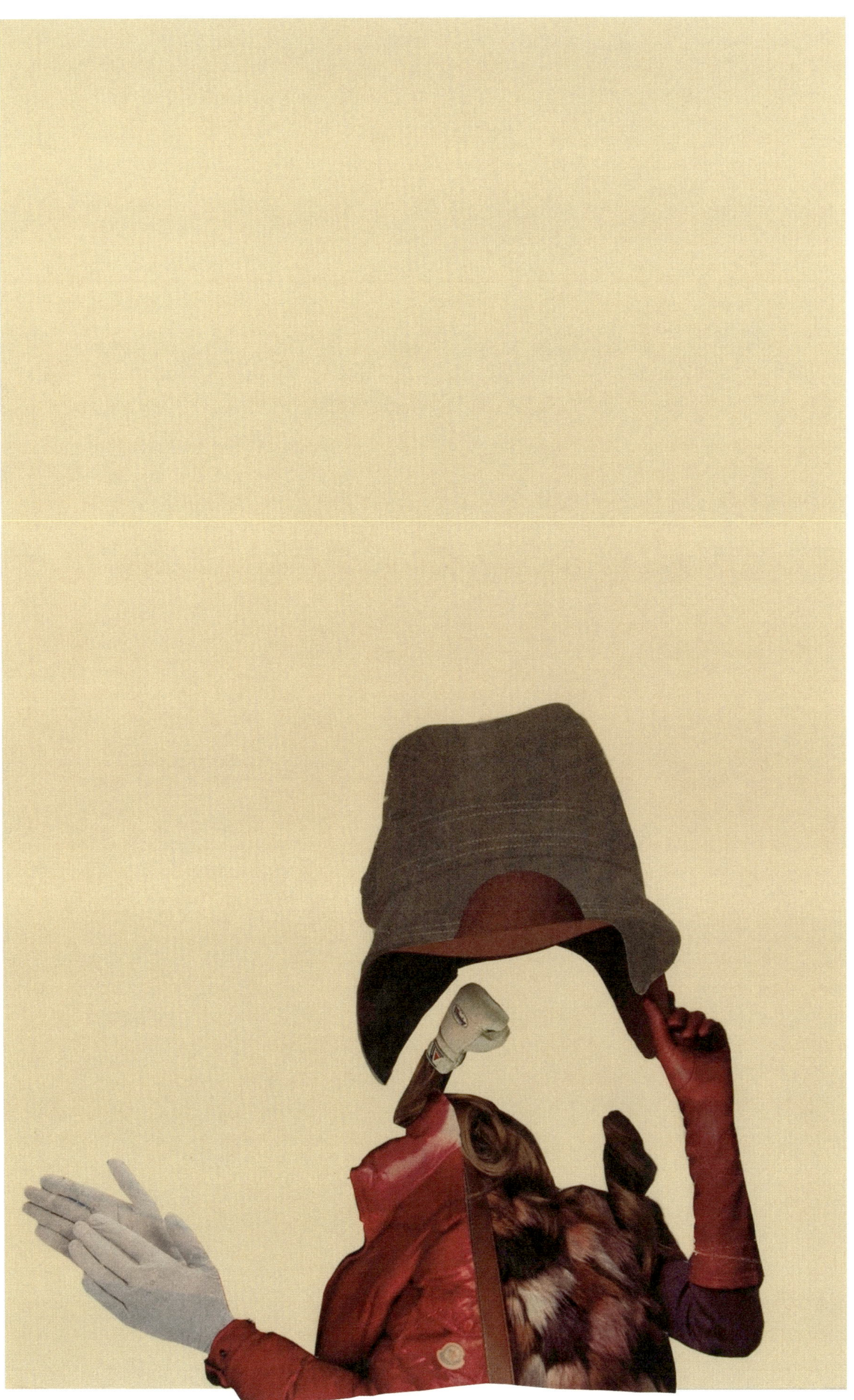

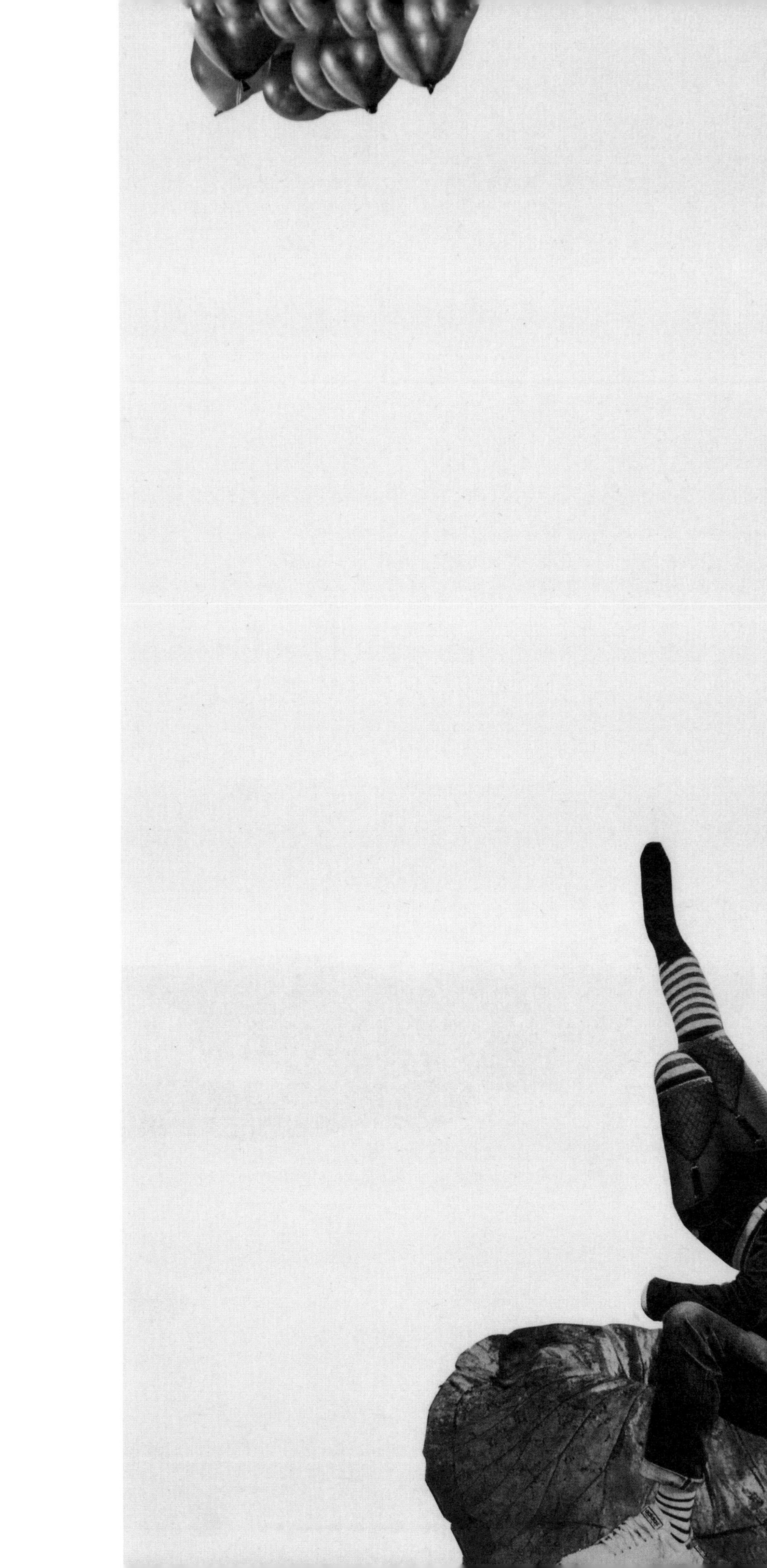

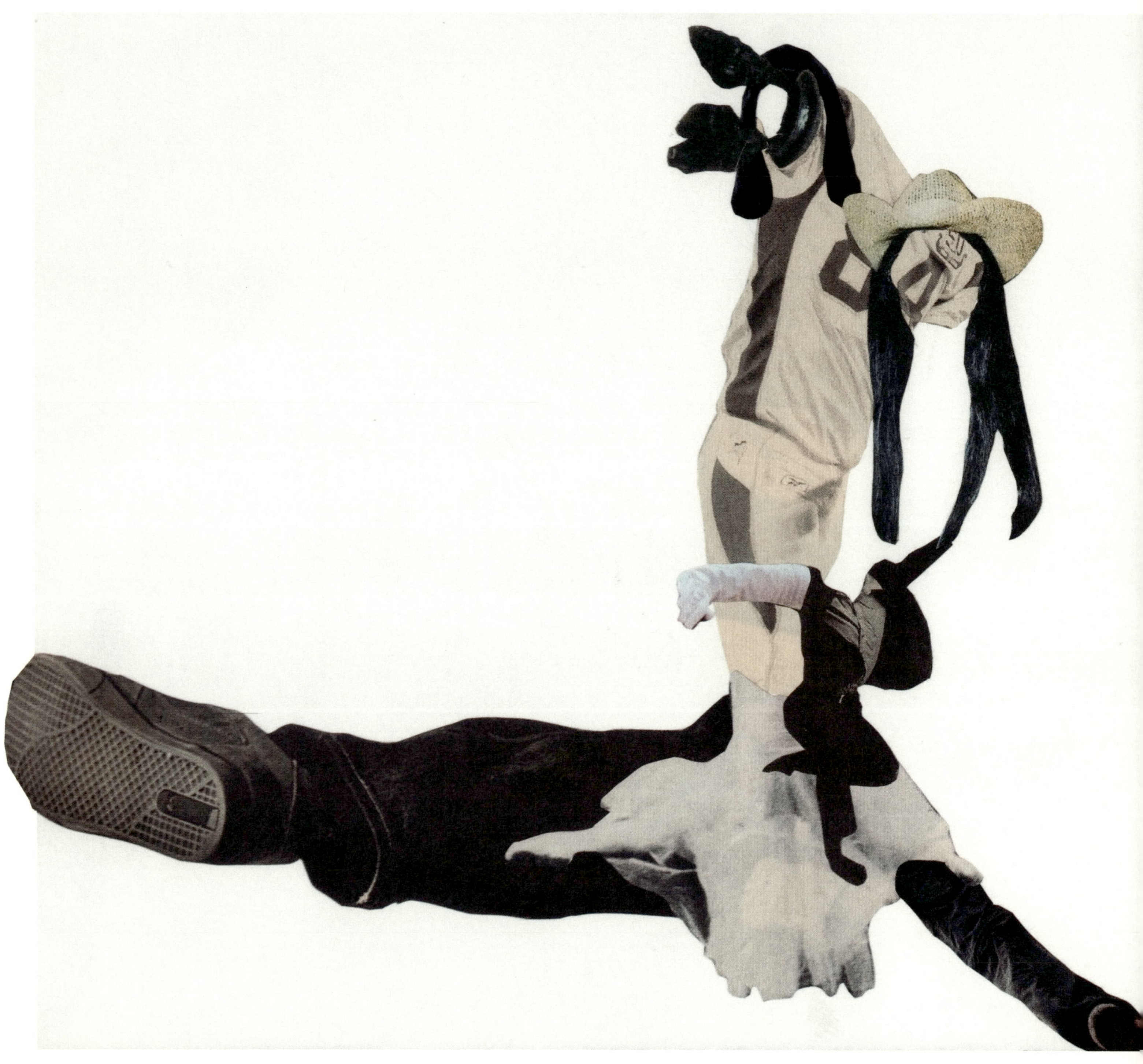

I can't speak much to time. In this world, there's no daylong, no yearlong, no orbiting of celestial bodies. There are hoodings, suitings, and unfurlings. In a larger sense, there is gradual emergence, too. The emergence of forms, assemblages, outfits even. And there was one strange emergence that ended everything.

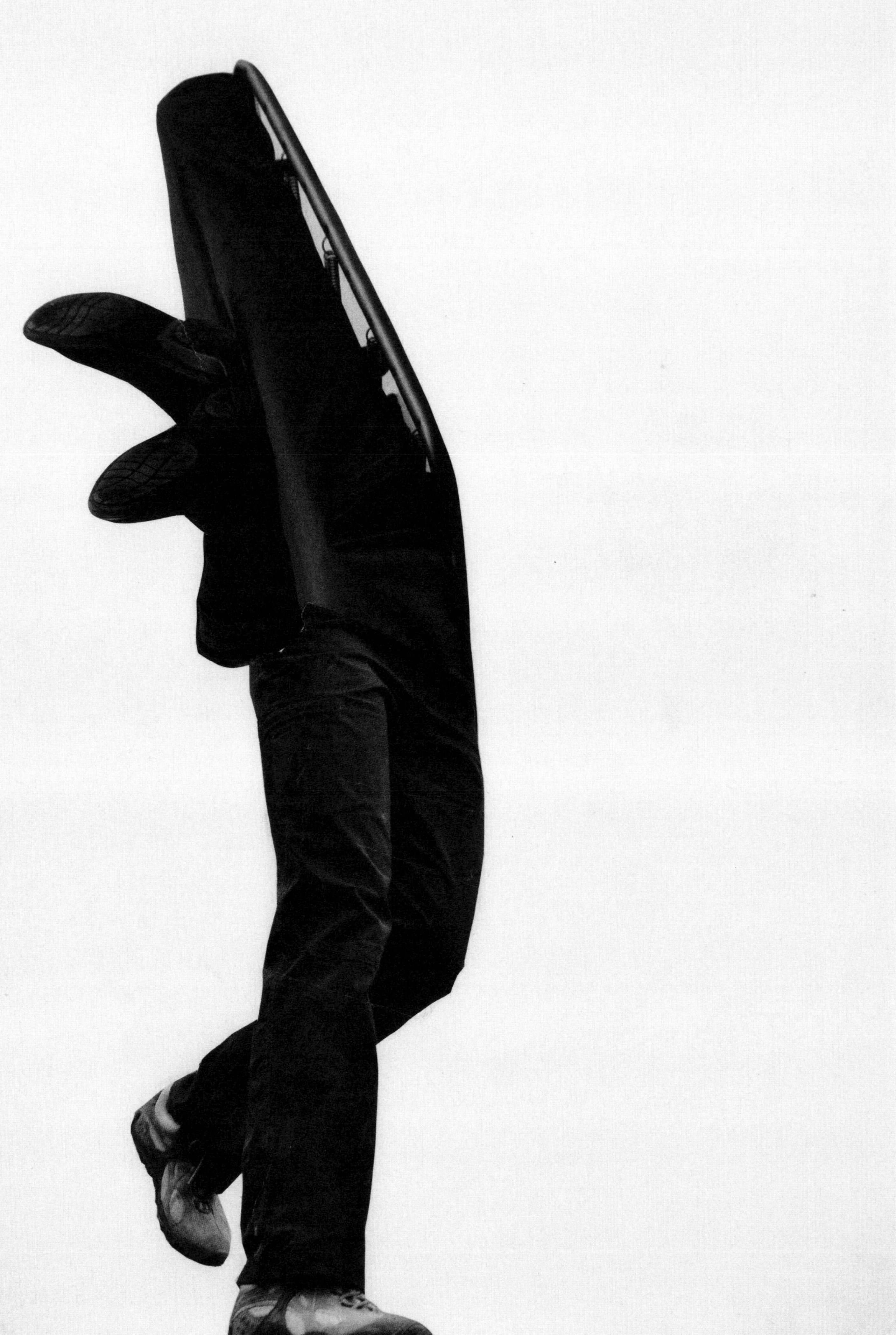

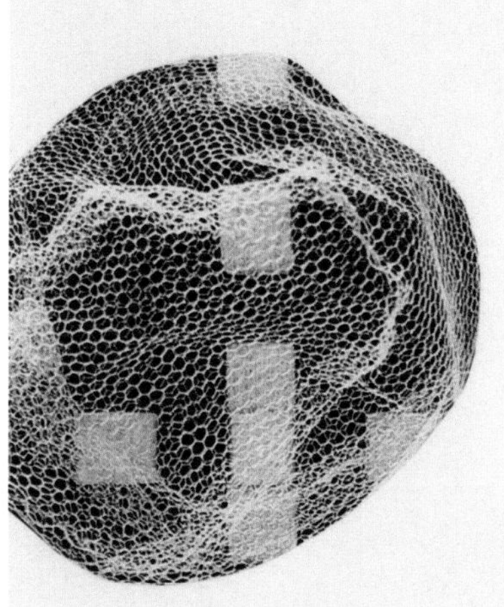

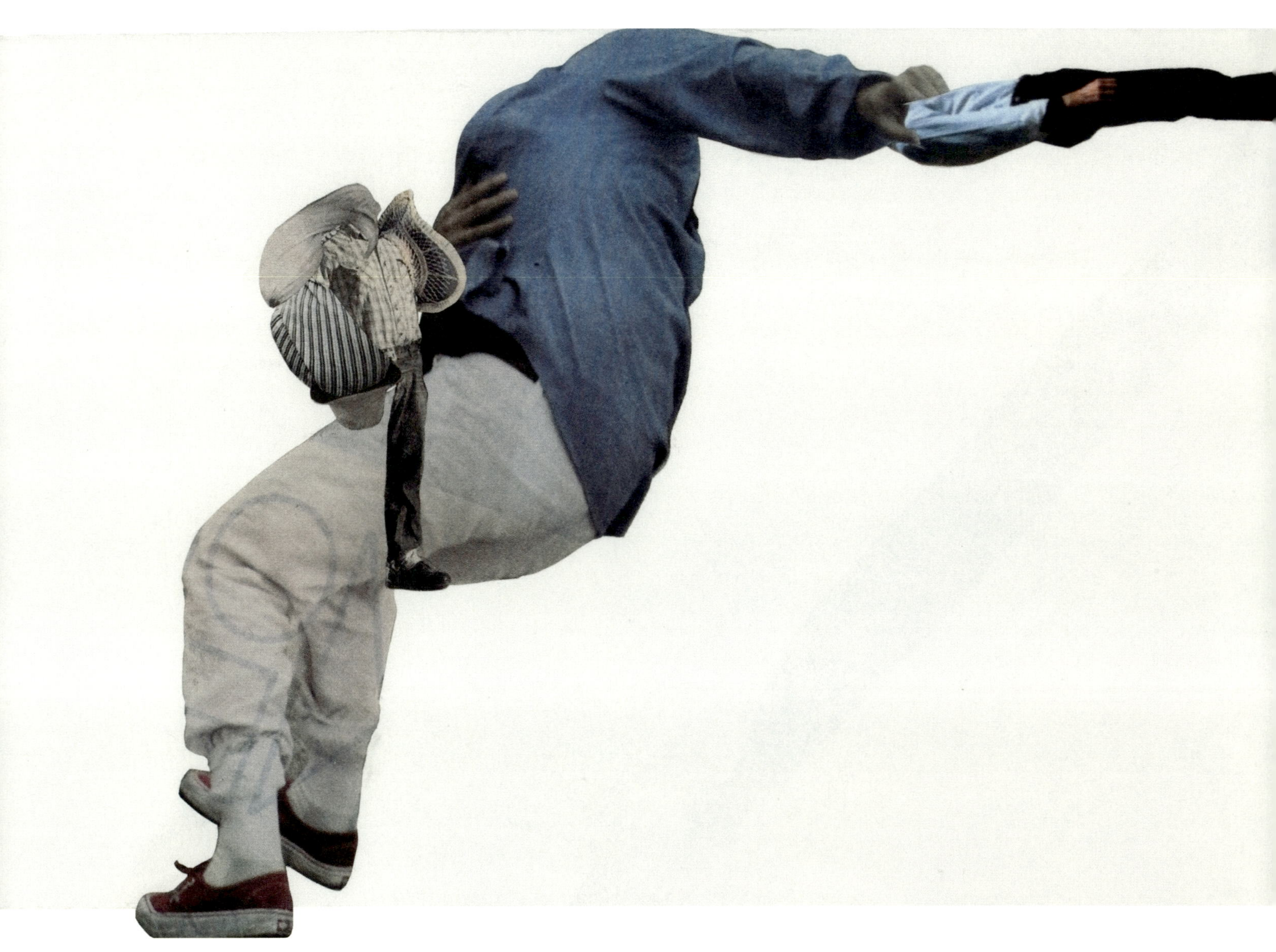

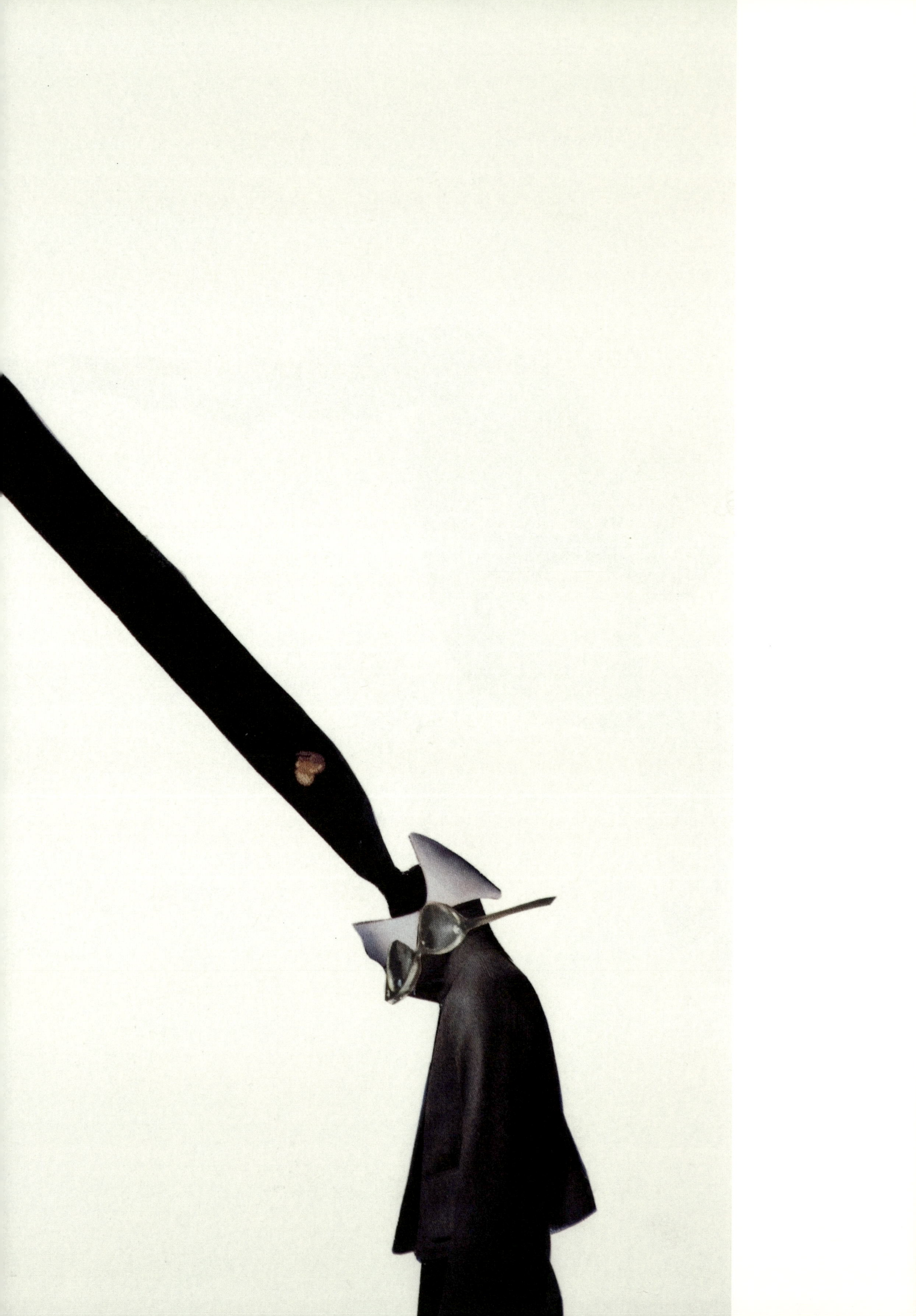

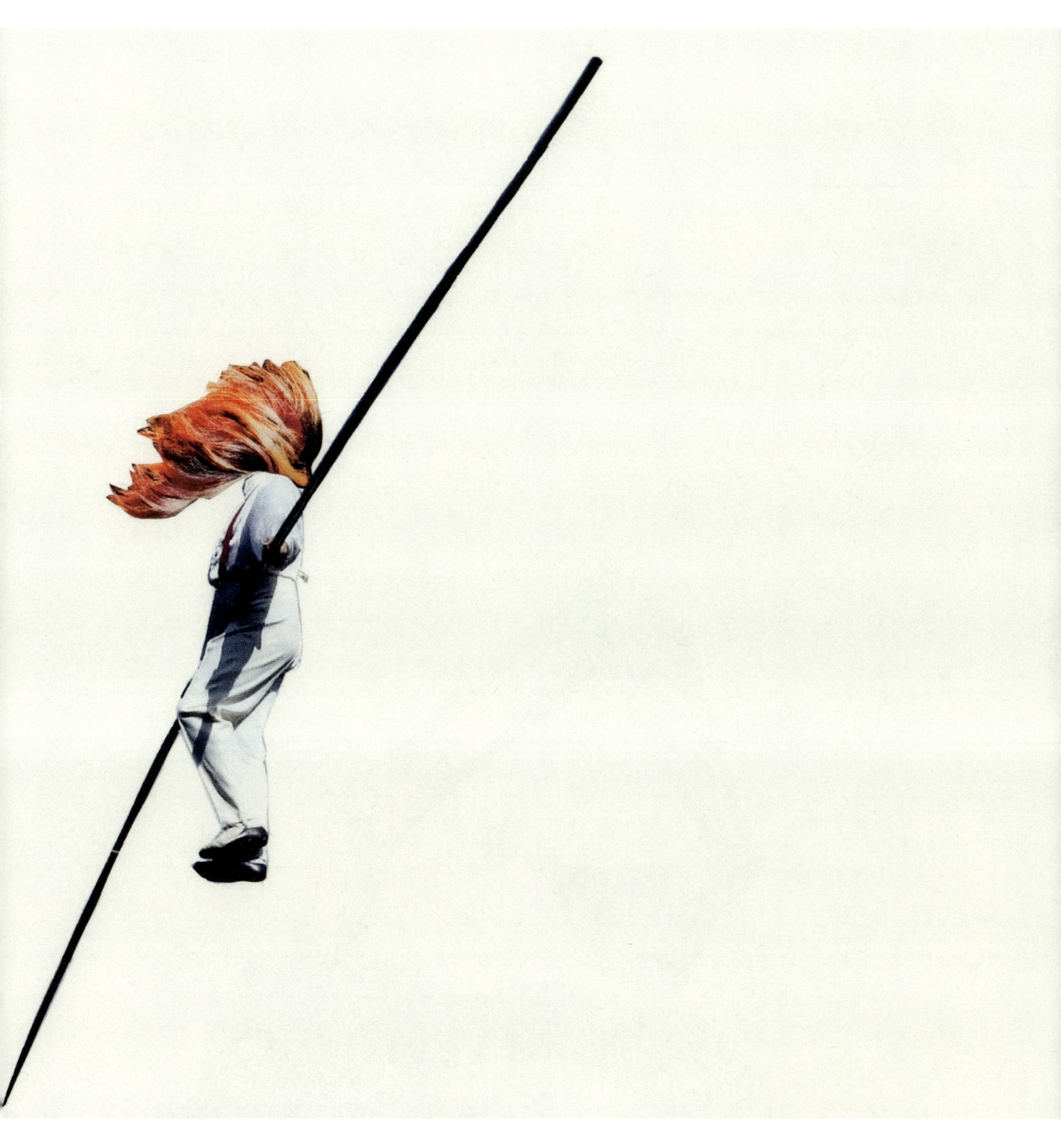

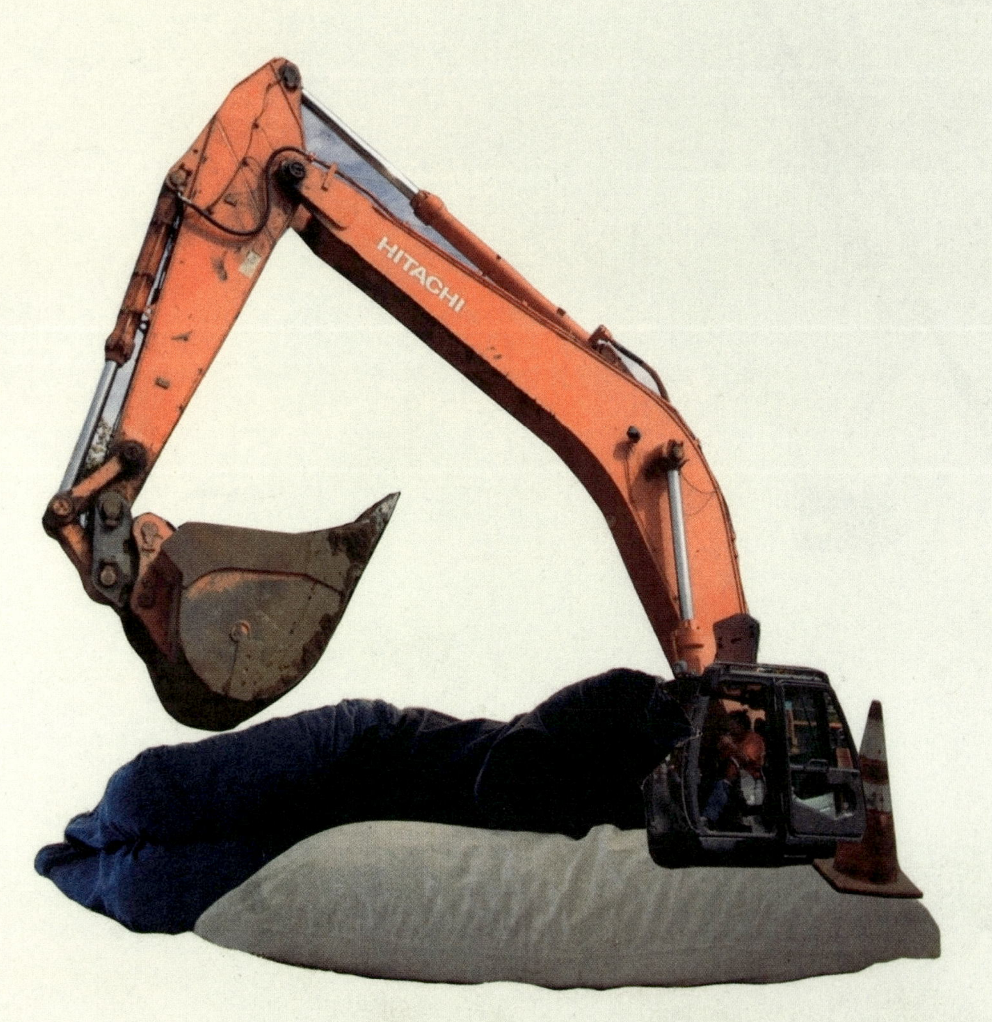
HITACHI

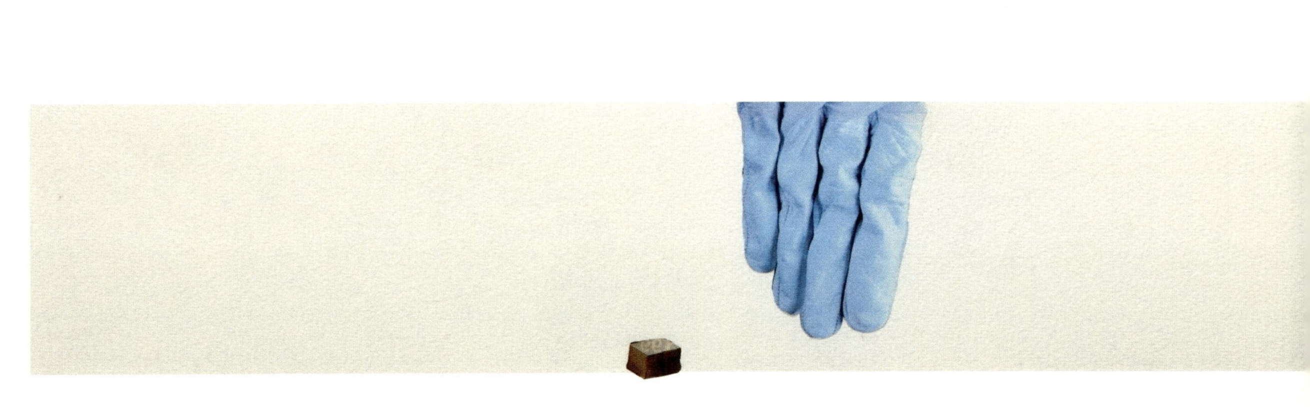

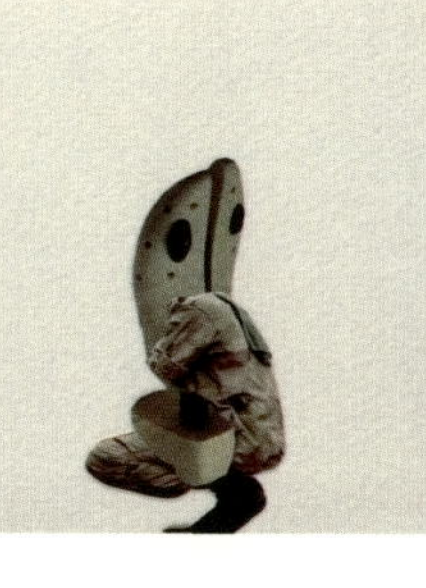

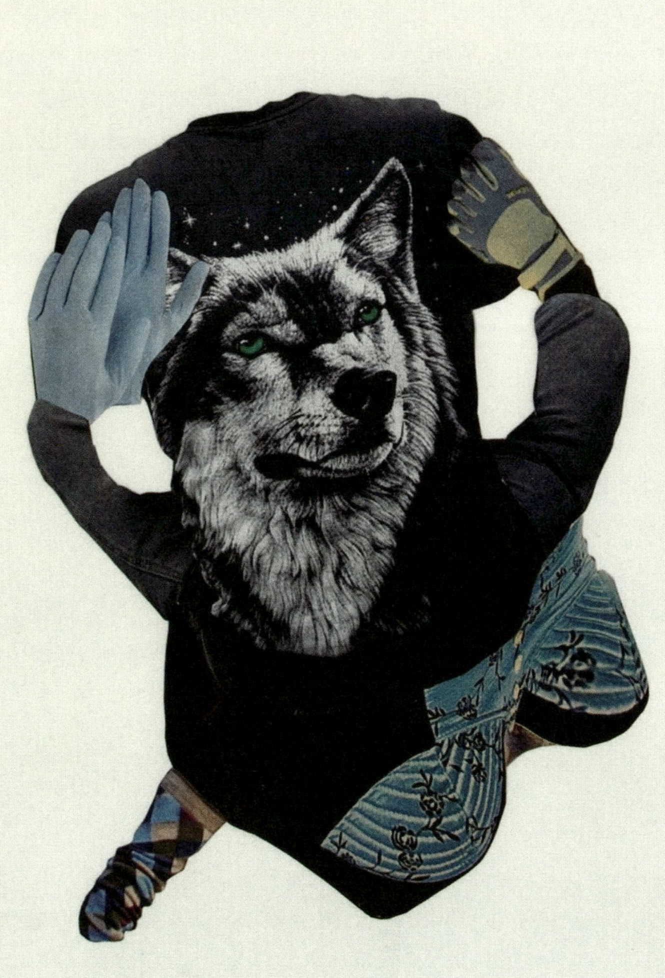

It was probably there from the beginning—a little bit of antimatter, imperceptible but *there*, and slowly spreading along with everything. When it started to take form, it wasn't comprehensible. It acted differently, but it was present and growing. Now I know what this other element was that didn't fit into any category. It was me.

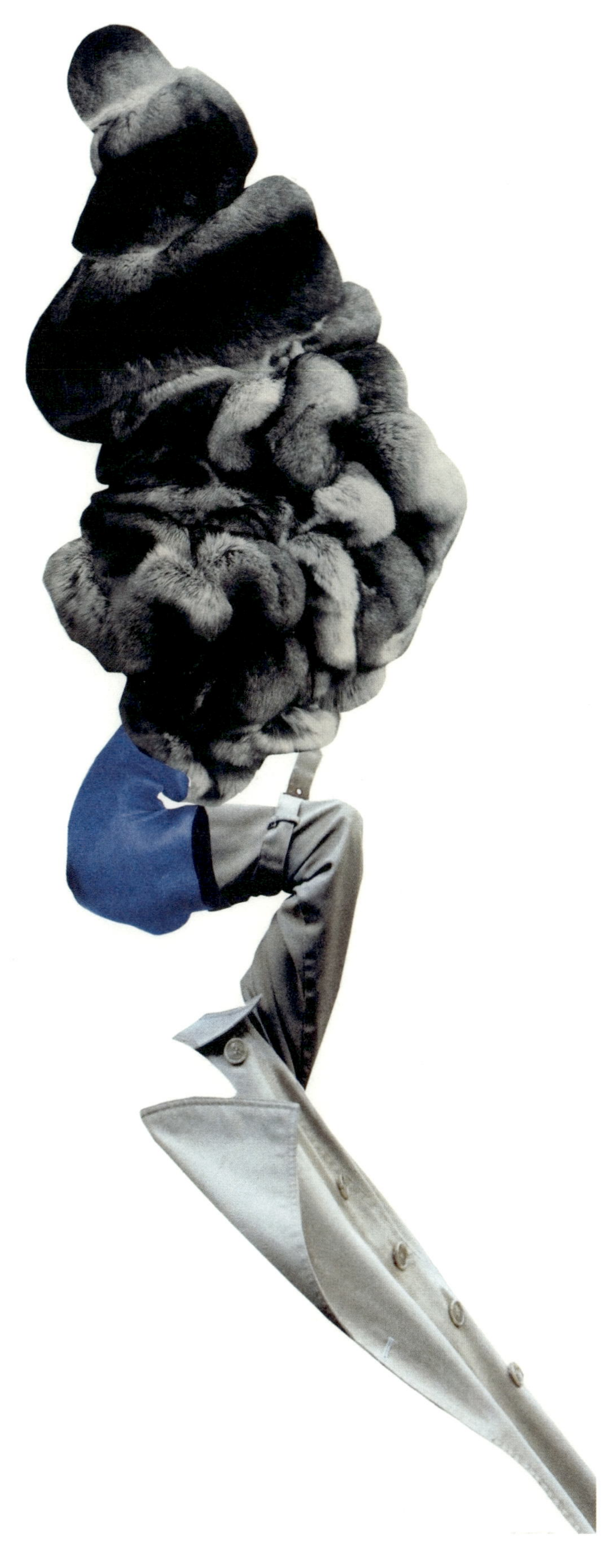

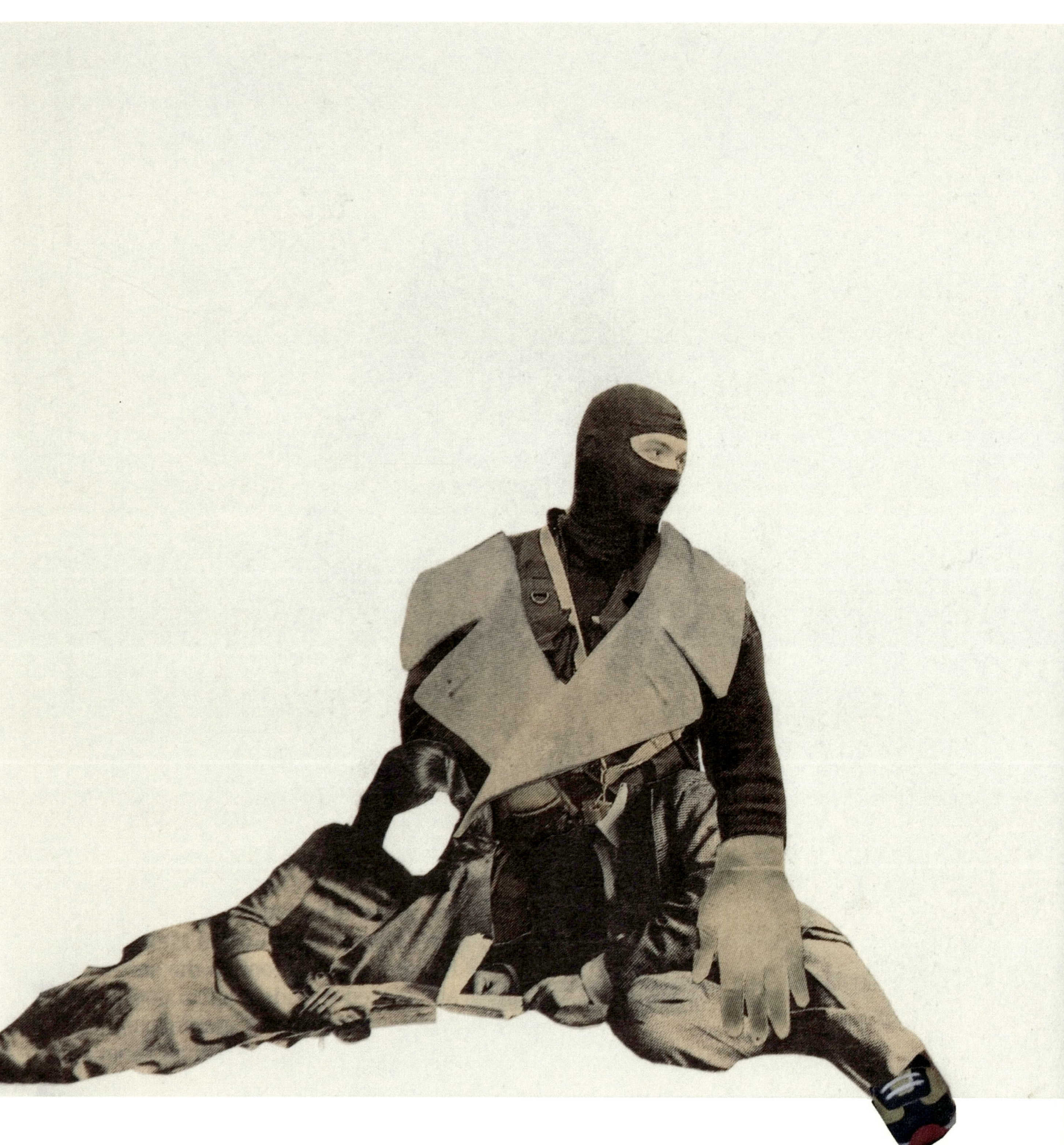

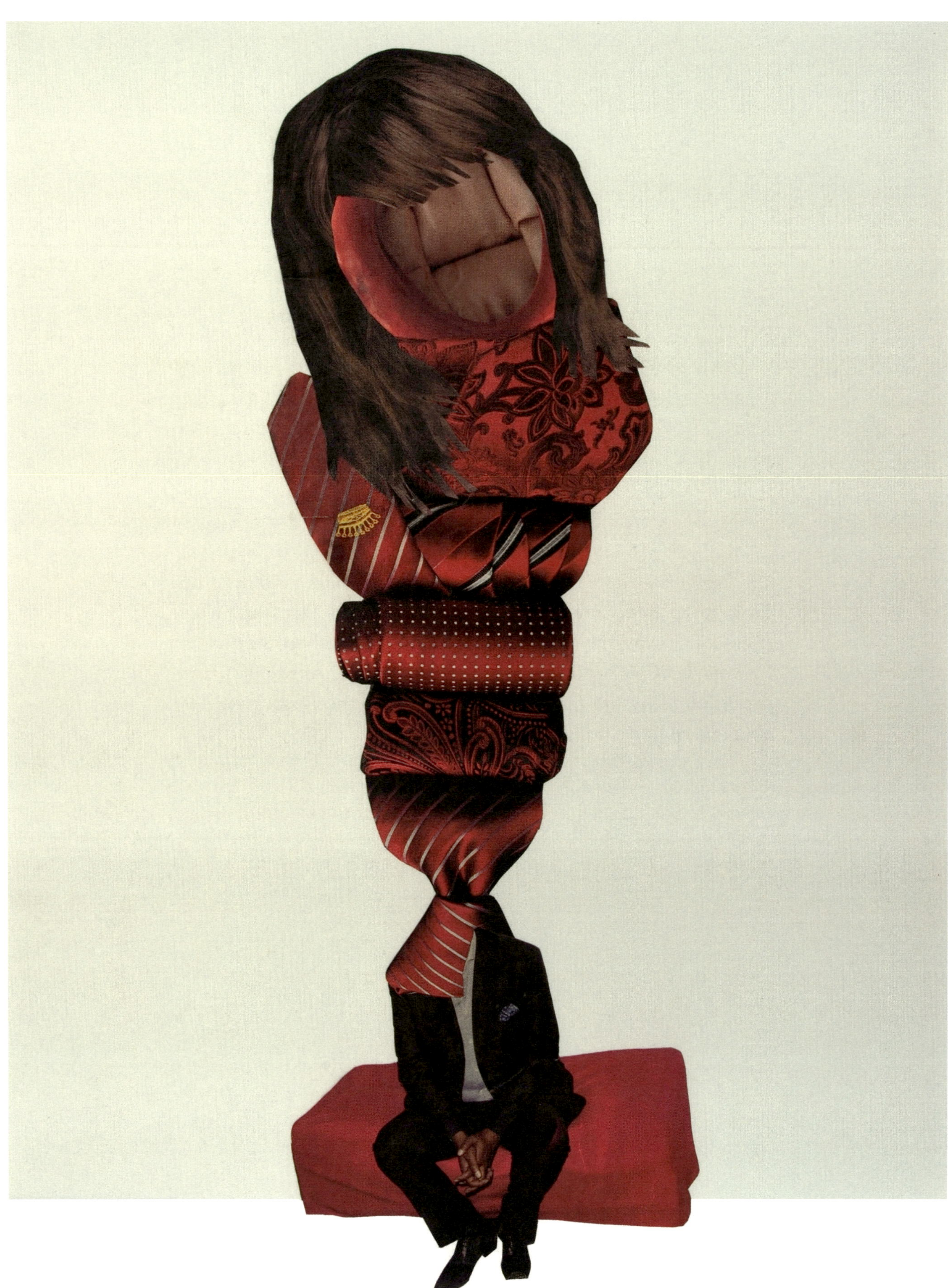

The separate me, the old enveloped me was showing up as a hand here, an ankle there. And by the time that eyes appeared, everything else began to fade. Clothing began to lose its violence and immensity. The tension, attraction, and repulsion in all the fibers seeped away. All that *was* grew still and hollow and finally receded.

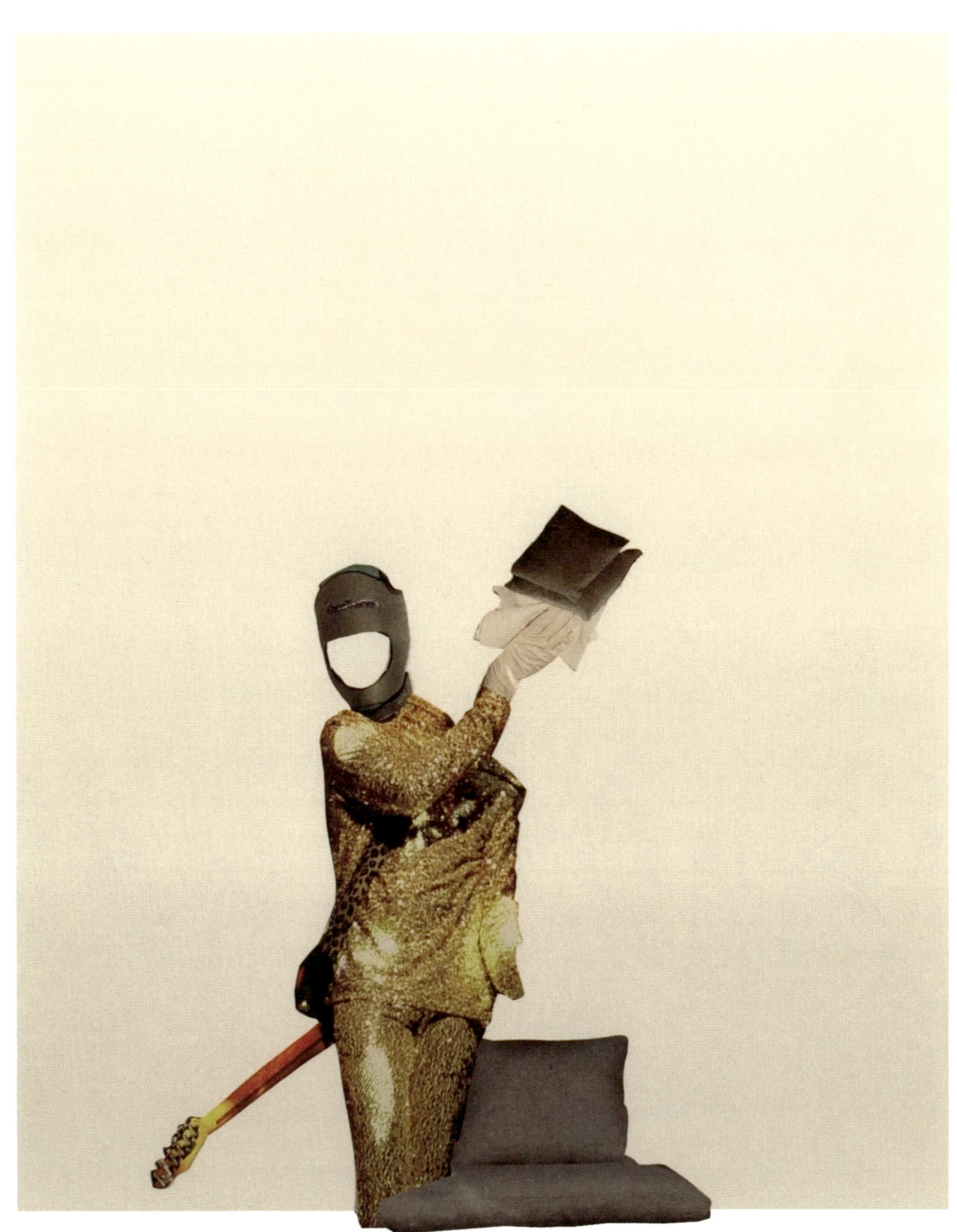

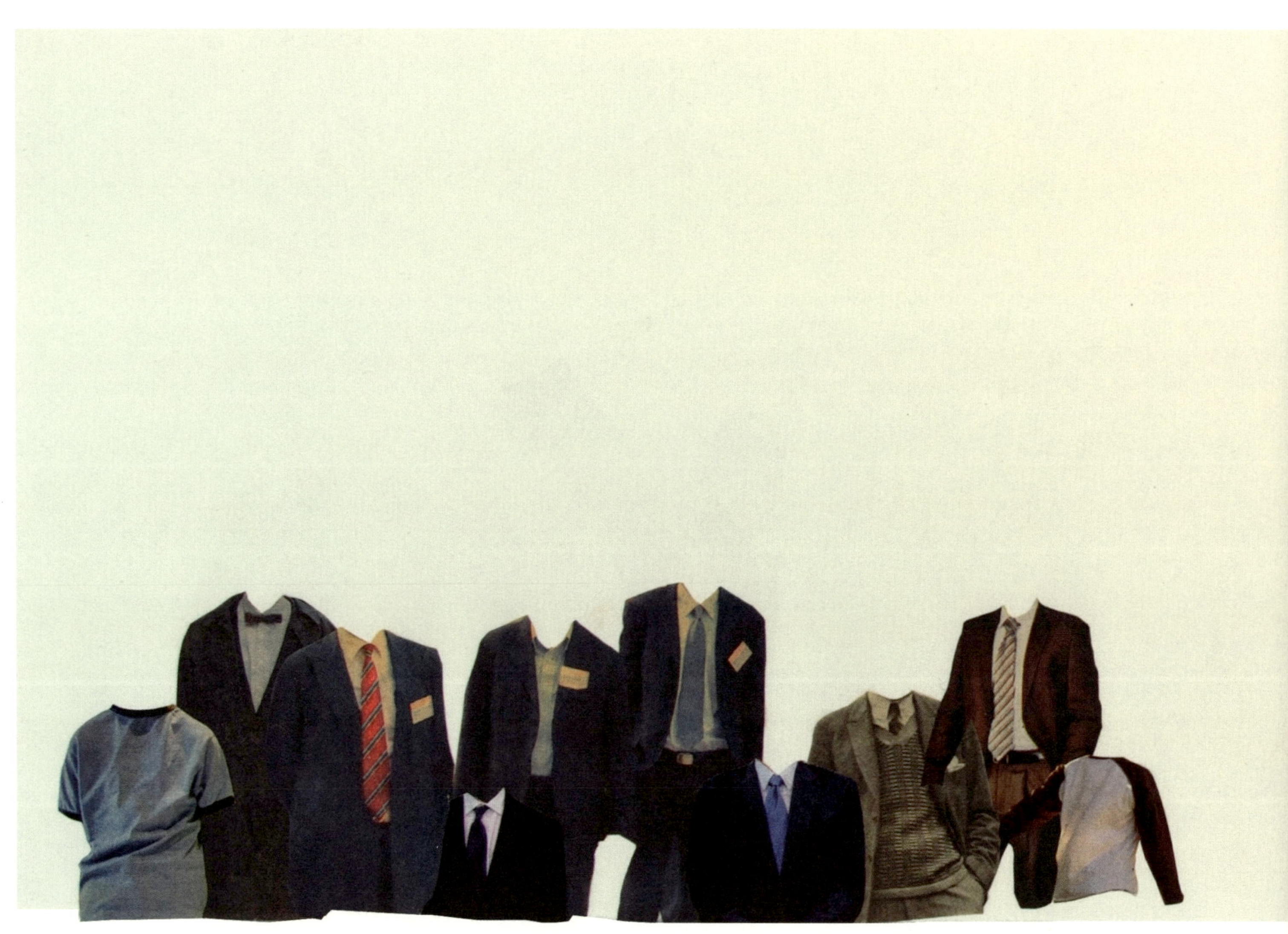

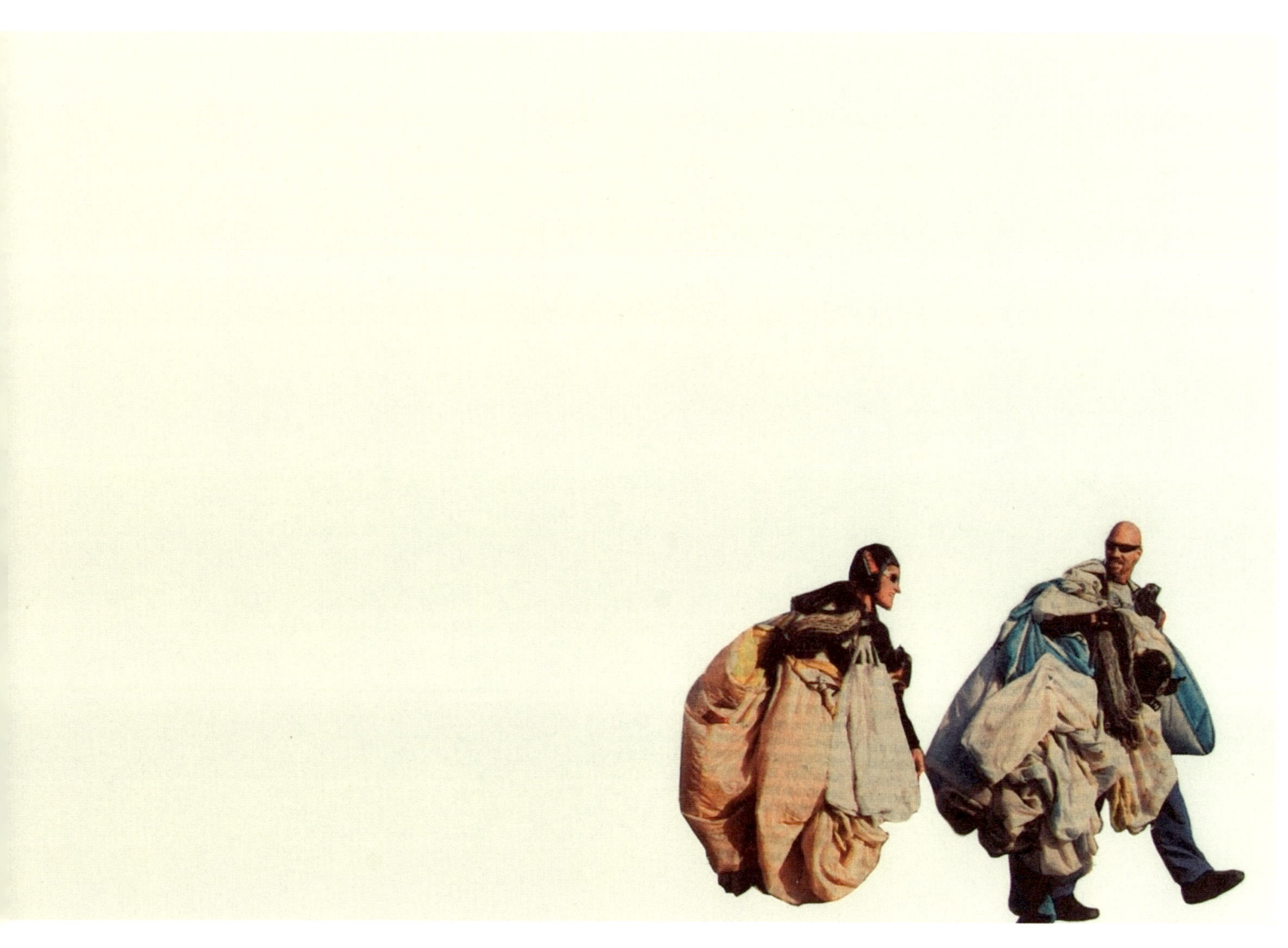

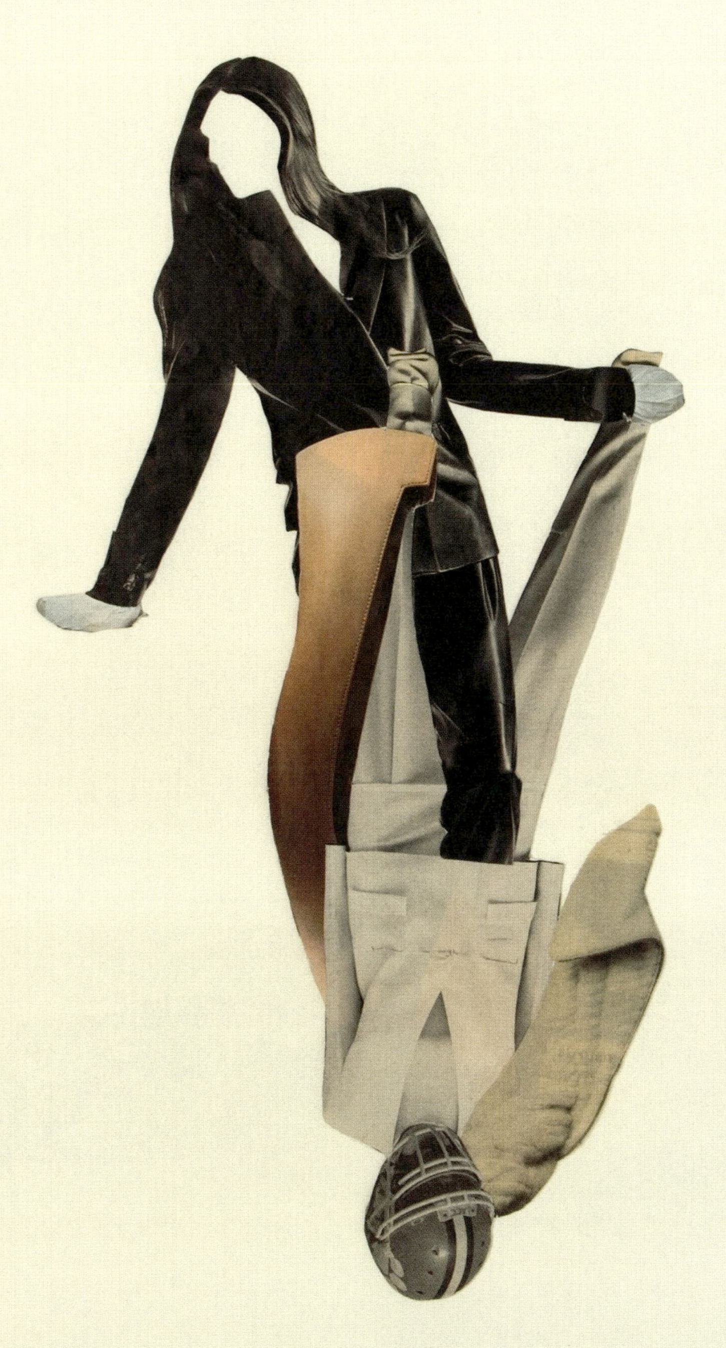

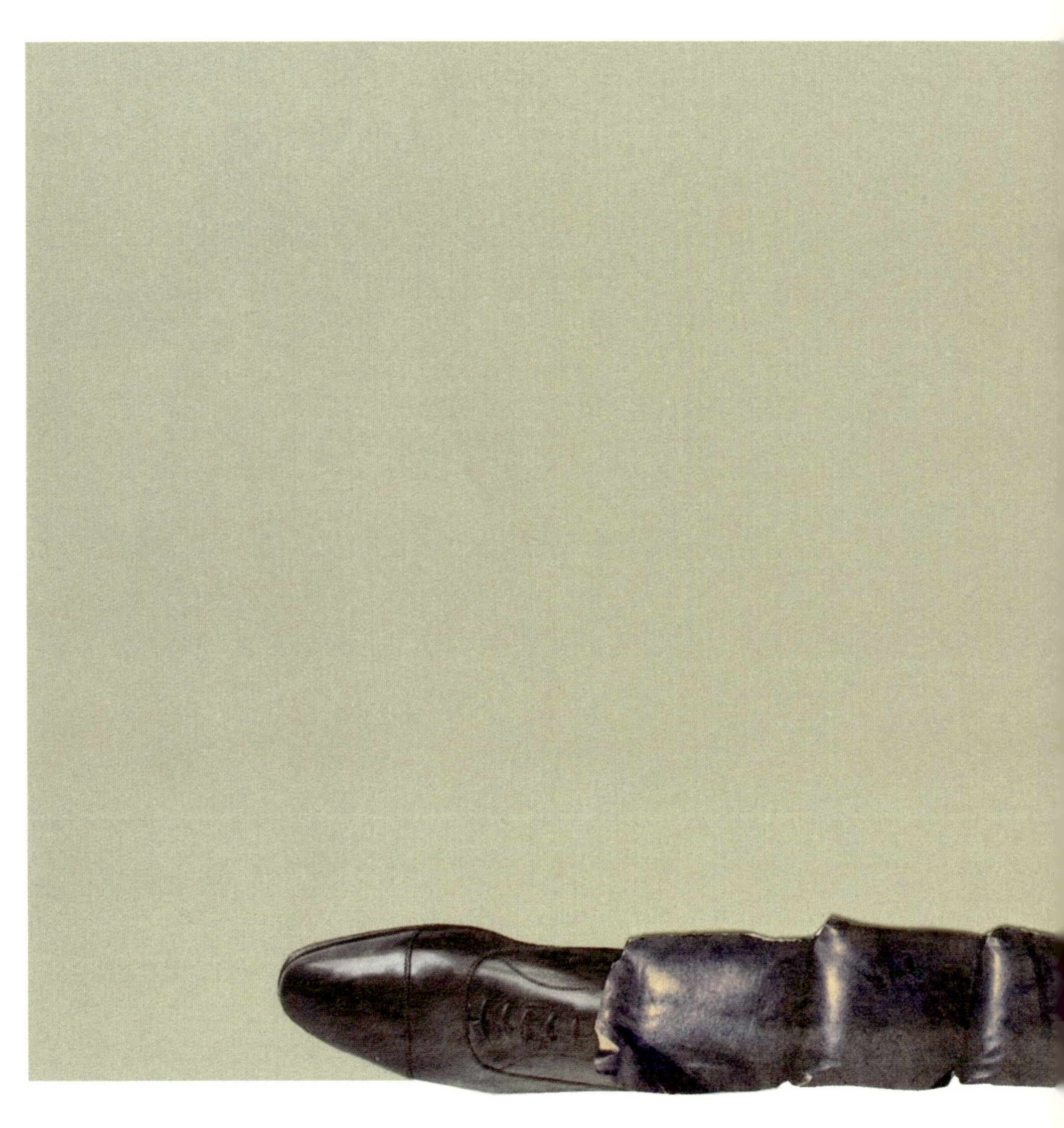

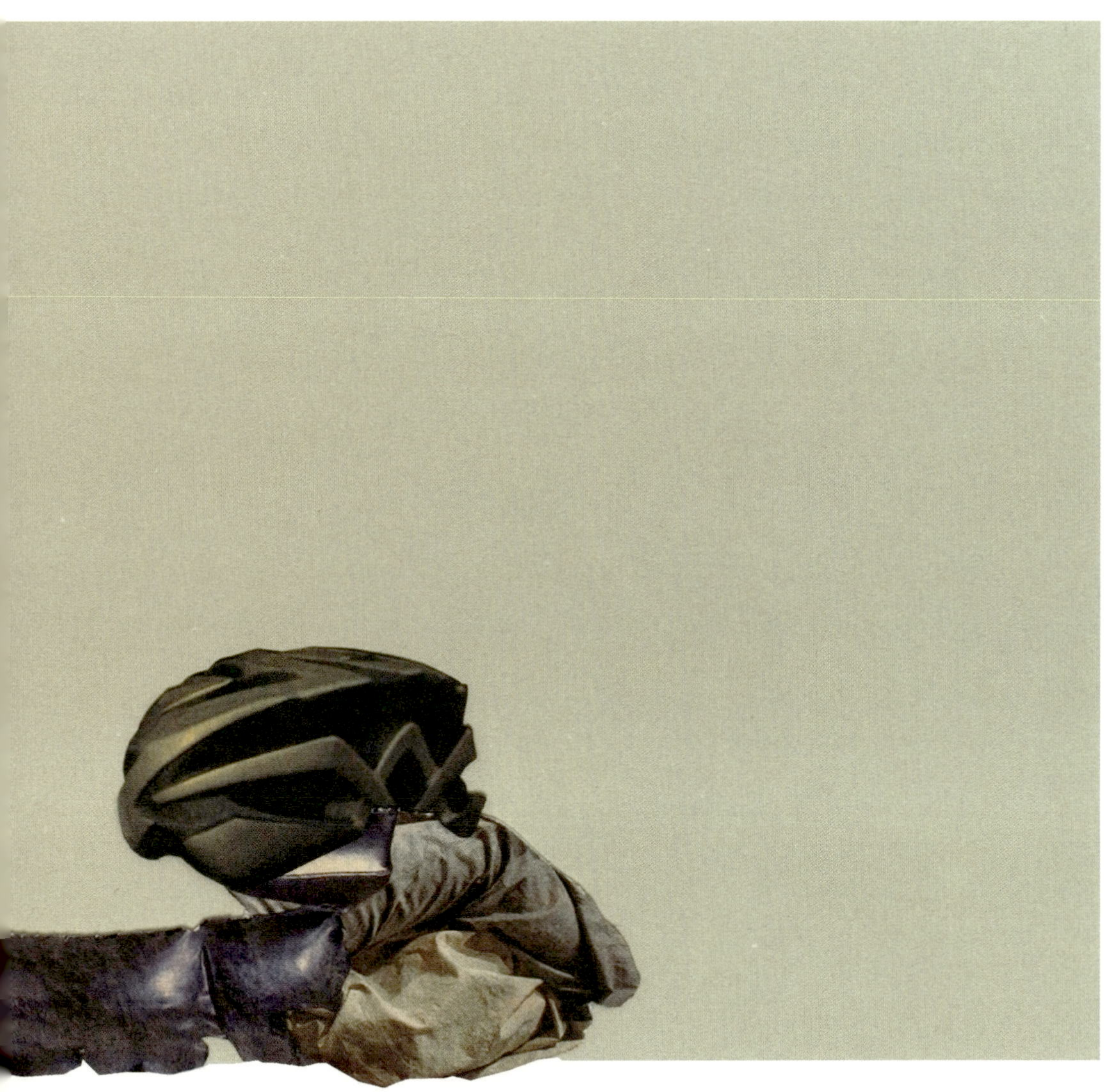

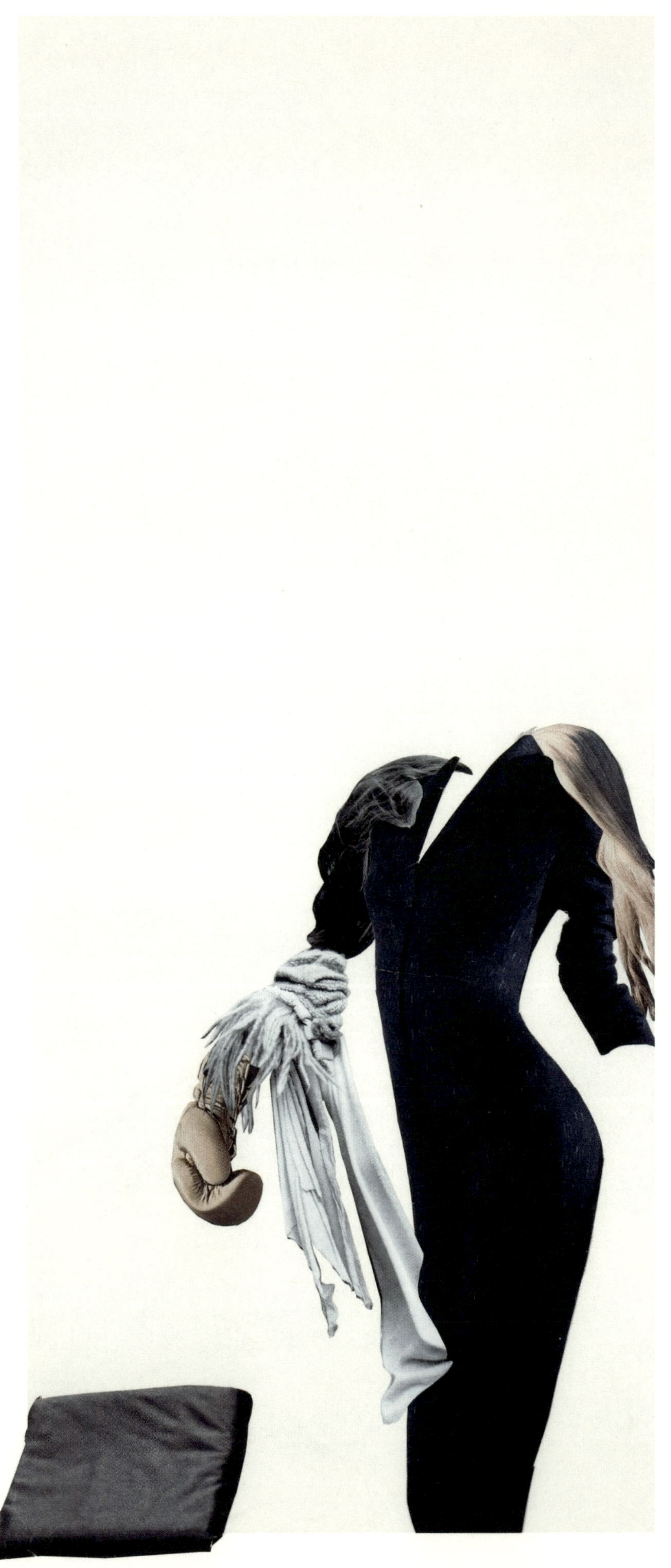

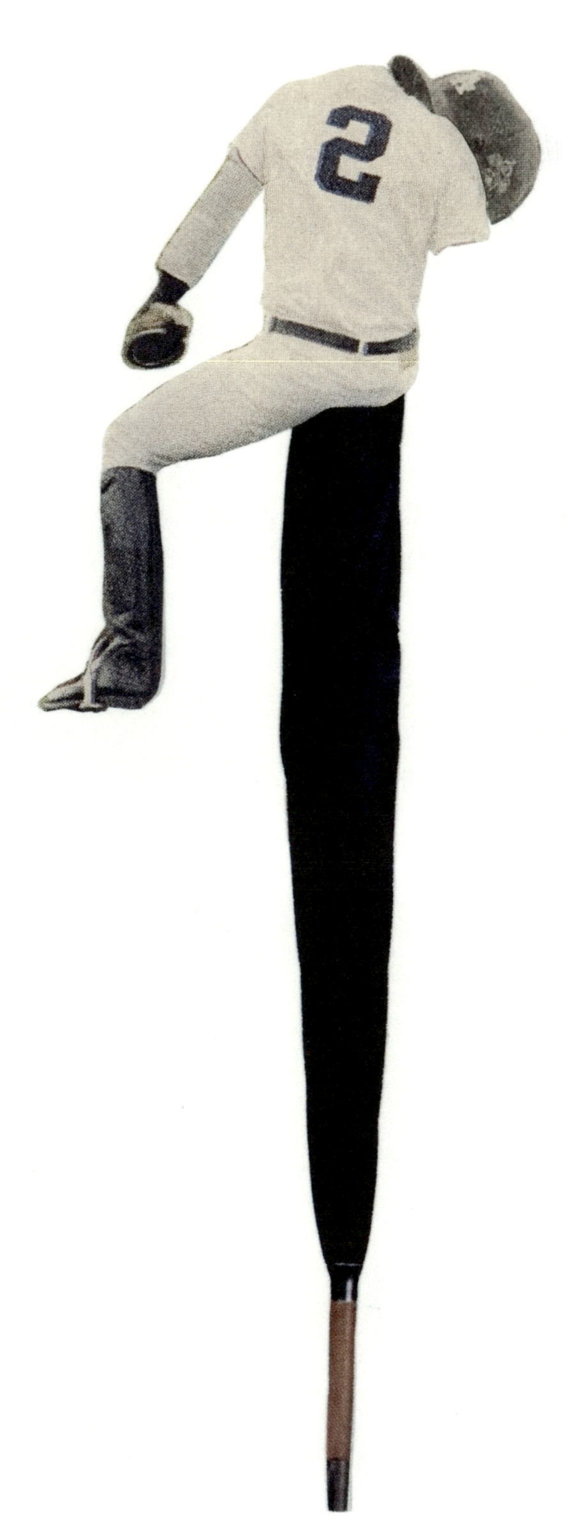

That world left me and I found myself back in the old world—
the world of pitch and tone, depth and plane, leg and bed,
blood and fear. I was told I had recovered. Now I put on
clothes and give talks like these. Neurologists everywhere
clamber to inspect and explain me. I ask each one the same
question and always get the same look. The question I ask
is *how do I get back to the other world?* The look they give is
the one you have right now.

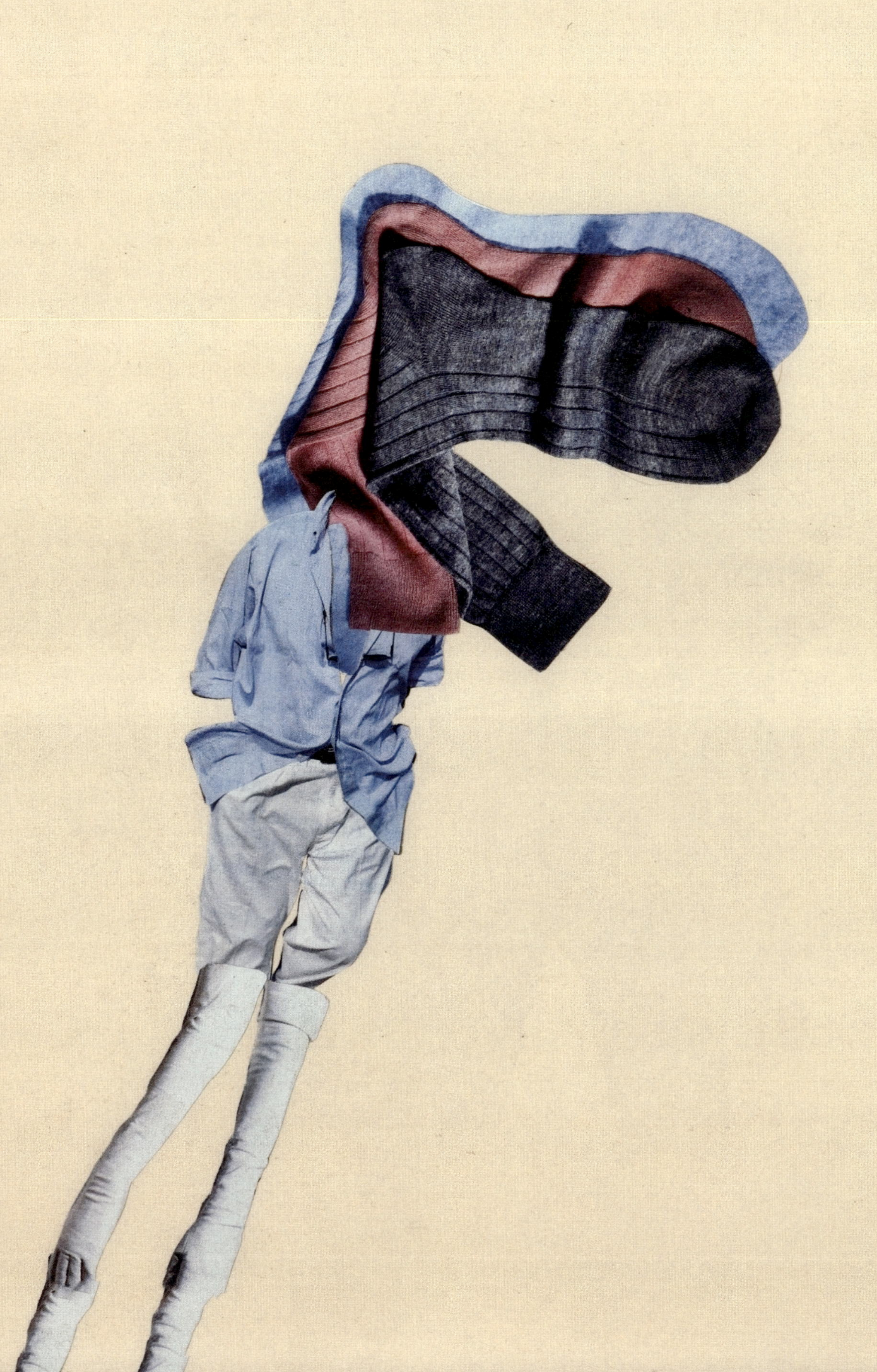

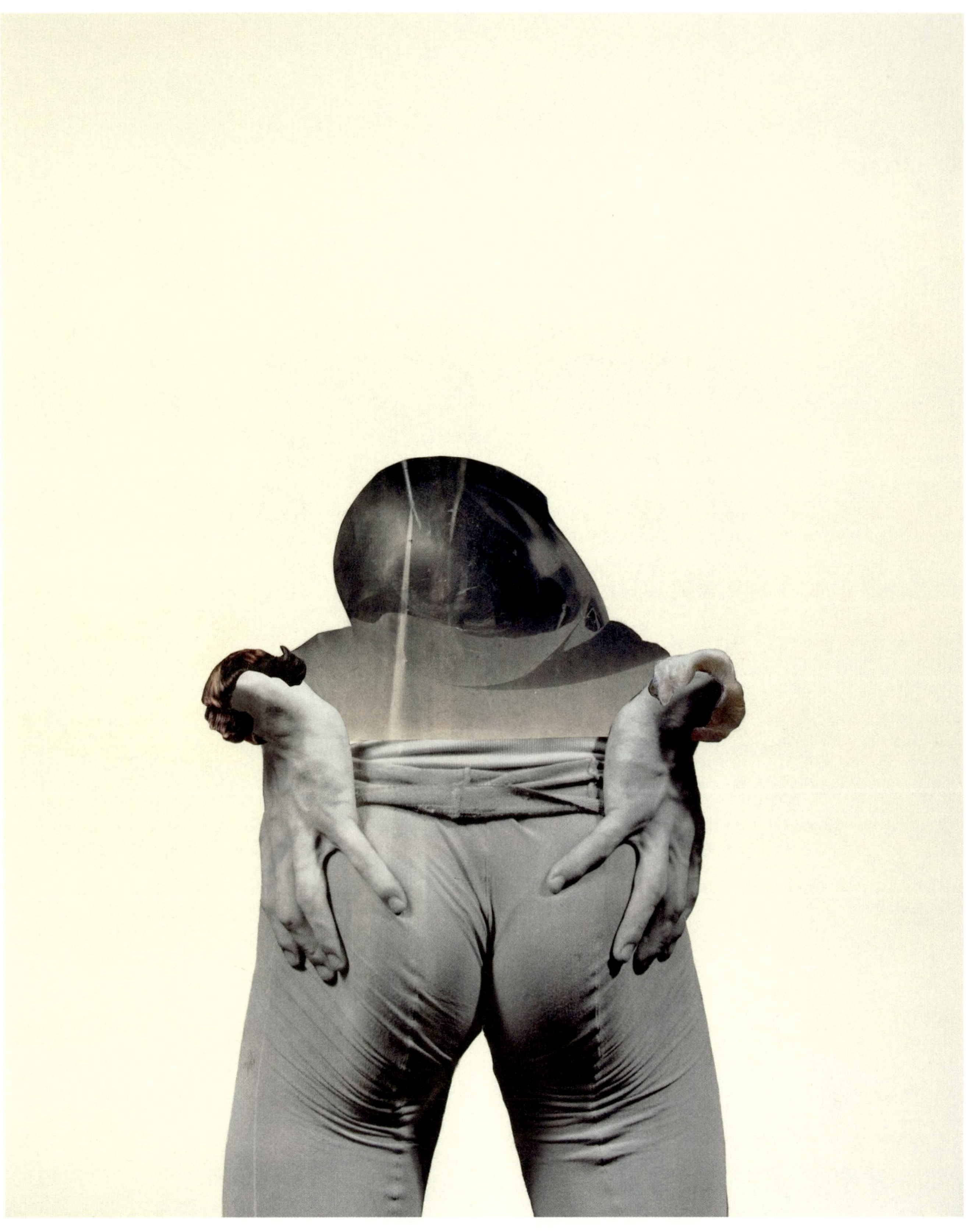

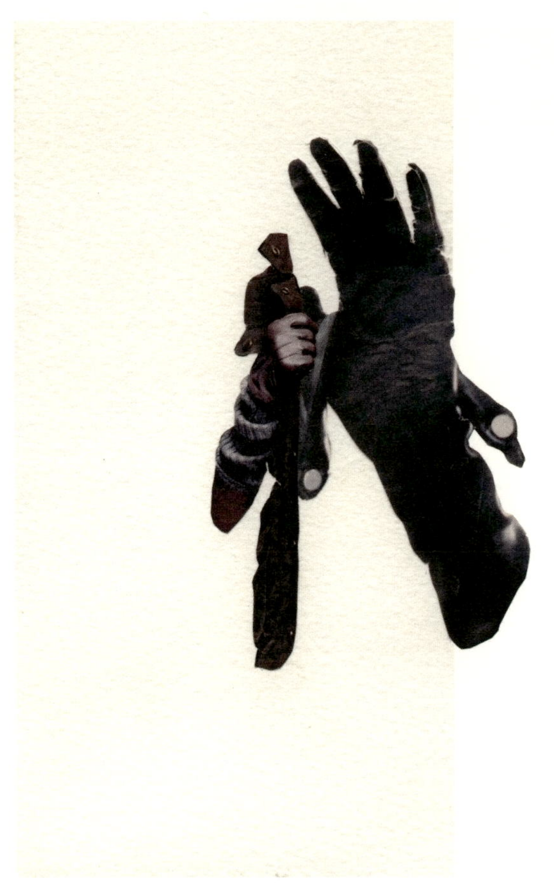

UNIFORMS
© 2013 Bettina Hubby and The Ice Plant

Edition of 750

All collages by Bettina Hubby

Text: "Always a Part That Pulls Away" © 2013 Dave Cull

Coordination: Jacques Marlow

Printed by The Avery Group at Shapco Printing Inc., Minneapolis
ISBN 978-0-9823653-9-7

Distributed in North America by Artbook | Distributed Art Publishers
www.artbook.com

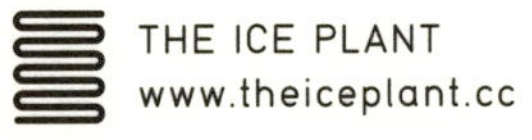 THE ICE PLANT
www.theiceplant.cc